Erin—
mas Bou always
have you & the
journez!

♡ Linda Kozack

REACHING THE SUMMIT: REFLECTIONS FOR THE JOURNEY

A Devotional Guide to Ponder as You Make
Your Way Through the Colorado 14ers

LINDA KOZACEK & LEIGH LEGERE

WESTBOW
PRESS®
A DIVISION OF THOMAS NELSON
& ZONDERVAN

WestBow Press books may be ordered through booksellers or by contacting:

WestBow Press
A Division of Thomas Nelson & Zondervan
1663 Liberty Drive
Bloomington, IN 47403
www.westbowpress.com
1 (866) 928-1240

Photos by Shawn Legere appear on pages 11, 22,
59, 68, 102, 105, 118, 136.
Photo by Donald S. Warner, III, appears on page 34
Photo by Greg Issinghoff appears page 145

Cover art created by Katie Mulder Creative

ISBN: 978-1-9736-8083-3 (sc)
ISBN: 978-1-9736-8084-0 (hc)
ISBN: 978-1-9736-8082-6 (e)

Library of Congress Control Number: 2019919705

Print information available on the last page.

WestBow Press rev. date: 01/07/2020

To our fellow sojourners—

Some of you may be seasoned hikers preparing for another 14er ascent, while others may never take such a serious hike. But as surely as you are breathing, you are on a journey. Most likely it has been filled with mountains and valleys, twists and turns, unmarked paths and missteps. On our own journeys, our paths have never been flat and straight. However, both of us have felt blessed—blessed to feel God's majesty on a summit, and equally blessed to see His reflection on water in a valley. He is *always* with us, if we only choose to look.

This book in an overflow of so many things...

- of coffee and smoothies from hours of pondering life and scriptures in a booth at our favorite coffee shop.
- of love, for those who are gone from our past and the kids and grandkids who are the promise of our future.
- of the support of our spouses who have encouraged and supported us on this journey.
- of blood, sweat, and tears—the blood of Jesus that we know was shed for us, the sweat of continually placing one foot in front of the other regardless of the path, and the tears that came from the perpetual realization that we are never alone—we are always and unconditionally loved.
- of overwhelming gratitude for the Search and Rescue team for heeding the call from a certain Garmin satellite phone.

We wrote this book for many reasons, but really we wanted to have a guidebook for our grandchildren for their future journeys—a little guidebook from their grammies, which includes a little wisdom and a lot of insight into the women we are—women who pace on the uphill, enjoy the view on the downhill, and who are always chasing whimsy.

CONTENTS

• •

Front Range
- Mount Bierstadt 2
- Mount Evans 6
- Grays Peak 8
- Longs Peak 11
- Pike's Peak 14
- Torreys Peak 17

Mosquito Range and Tenmile Range
- Mount Bross 22
- Mount Democrat 25
- Mount Lincoln 28
- Mount Sherman 31
- Quandary Peak 34

Sawatch Range
- Mount Antero 38
- Mount Belford 41
- Mount Columbia 44
- Mount Elbert 47
- Mount Harvard 50
- Mount of the Holy Cross 53
- Huron Peak 56
- La Plata Peak 59

- Mount Massive 62
- Missouri Mountain 65
- Mount Oxford..68
- Mount Princeton..71
- Mount Shavano..74
- Tabeguache Peak..77
- Mount Yale..80

Sangre de Cristo Range
- Blanca Peak..84
- Crestone Needle..87
- Crestone Peak 90
- Culebra Peak 93
- Ellingwood Point 95
- Humboldt Peak..98
- Kit Carson Peak/Challenger Point 102
- Little Bear Peak 105
- Mount Lindsey 108

Elk Mountains
- Capitol Peak 112
- Castle Peak 115
- Maroon Peak 118
- North Maroon Peak 121
- Pyramid Peak 124
- Snowmass Mountain 127

San Juan Mountains
- El Diente Peak..130
- Mount Eolous..133
- Handies Peak 136
- Redcloud Peak 139
- San Luis Peak..142
- Mount Sneffels..145
- Sunlight Peak..148

- Sunshine Peak...150
- Uncompahgre Peak...153
- Wetterhorn Peak...156
- Mount Wilson...159
- Wilson Peak...162
- Windom Peak 165

FRONT RANGE

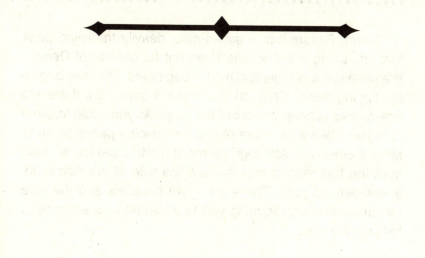

MOUNT BIERSTADT

Mount Bierstadt is a seven-mile, heavily trafficked peak that sits along the Guanella Pass not far outside of Denver. We were told it is a great climb for beginners. The hike begins by dipping down. Early on you cross a creek, but there are boardwalks to keep you out of the bogs. As you begin to climb to higher elevations, more of the surrounding peaks begin to show themselves. Although we never made it that far, we read from the trail reports that the last half-mile of the hike lacks a well-defined path. There are more boulders and the hike becomes steeper, requiring you to do some mild scrambling towards the end.

Do not call to mind the former things
Or ponder things of past.
Behold, I will do something new
Now it will spring forth;
Will you not be aware of it?
I will even make a roadway in the wilderness,
Rivers in the desert.
Isaiah 43:18-19

Listening to my friend describe her love of hiking 14ers made me want to experience it firsthand. I love being outdoors; I love being active; and I wanted to challenge myself physically in ways that I never had before. I had just come through a season of multiple valleys where, over the last four decades of my life,

2

one loved one after another was laid to final rest. However, this particular summer was a mountaintop experience for my husband and me. In the span of a few months, we celebrated the marriage of our youngest daughter followed by the birth of our first grandchild to our oldest daughter. This season of joy and celebration was new territory for the two of us as only one year earlier we had both buried family members after long fought illnesses. We wanted to mark this new season in a significant way as we were heading into our 50s.

I trained harder for this climb than I have ever trained before. The time I spent training gave me hours to reflect on my life and why this hike was so important to me. I didn't tell a lot of people my plan because I was too afraid of failing. After forty years of limitations due to problematic knees, I was afraid my body would not cooperate. Although I had been given some new hardware—a knee replacement—the years of limited activity had taken a toll on my heart. So I quietly persisted with a small band of encouragers cheering me on.

My husband and I chose Bierstadt because we had been told it was a great "starter" climb. We gave ourselves a few days to acclimate to the altitude and headed out for the hike well before dawn. We were excited and nervous as we set out hand in hand, not quite sure what to expect. The first few hours went great, but as we gained altitude, it became more difficult. We walked for hours, but it seemed to take forever because of all the breaks I needed to catch my breath. My husband kept encouraging me, and we kept going until it became a challenge to know if we should stop or continue on. And if we stopped, at what point was the right point *to* stop? We didn't want to miss out on anything.

Suddenly, we both got to a point where we looked at each other and instinctively knew this was it. We could go no further. We stepped off the path and found a somewhat private spot and sat on some rocks. I was sobbing, ashamed and frustrated that I had not been able to make it to the top. After a few minutes, his eyes misted as well, but for a different reason. He told me to catch my breath and look out at the view to see how far we had come.

From what I am told, Mount Bierstadt is one of the few 14ers where you can see your path from the entire hike. That moment on that rock gave us pause to reflect on the path we had been on for so long, a path that had been really tough on our hearts for many, many years. We had made it to a point where we were on a peak, literally and figuratively. From our position, we could finally look back and reflect on the path we had been on, appreciating how far we had come, while also enjoying the beautiful view of where we were sitting at this point in our lives. We never did make it to the summit, but we left that day with a renewed sense of joy. We experienced our own mountaintop after walking through so many valleys and were anticipating the remainder of our journey that was yet to come.

Father, we thank You for bringing us out of the valleys to experience Your glory on the mountaintop moments of our lives. Let us not spend too much time focused on how far we have come; rather, let us give glory to the one who has brought us out of the valley and gives us hope in anticipation of the journey that is yet to come. In Jesus' Name, Amen.

Date of Hike:

Climbing Party:

Notes:

MOUNT EVANS

•••

Almost immediately after setting foot on the trail for the backside of Mount Evans, we encountered a group of twenty-somethings. They did not have a map and were having trouble figuring out their route on the less-traveled west side of the mountain. After asking multiple questions, my husband handed over our map to the eager group. We had planned a different route, but both were highlighted, making route-finding easier. However, without the map, we got off route several times. While lacking a map complicated our hike, it made the other group's hike less difficult. Sometimes helping others burdens us. In this case, we felt it was important to carry that burden. Recently, I was reminded of that hike. While looking over my husband's neatly stacked pile of items for his next climb, I spotted his small Bible he always packs and it dawned on me—we should have given that to the group along with the Evans map. It is the ultimate path finder. We try to carry an extra copy of our intended route now. I truly hope our small act of kindness resulted in a successful first 14ers hike, instilling a love of hiking to a rookie group.

Calling to those who pass by,
Who are making their paths straight:
"Whoever is naïve, let him turn in here"
Proverbs 9:15

Isn't it a great feeling when we can share the Good News, especially with someone who may be wandering off the trail? We never know when we will find ourselves in a situation where we can share our map or point someone back to true north when they are lost. It might be with someone we are walking with daily, a friend who has lost their way or a stranger we meet on a mountain hike. We may think we are just "sharing a map," but in reality, our actions could put someone on the course that could change the ultimate direction of their life. When that person gets back on track and makes it to the mountaintop, witnessing the indescribable view, we pray they say, "God reigns!"

Dear Heavenly Father, show me the opportunities where I can share the Gospel in a way that can be understood for those who need to hear. Guide my words so that the one who hears is drawn to You. In Jesus' Name, Amen.

Date of Hike:

Climbing Party:

Notes:

7

GRAYS PEAK

●●●

Most 14er mountaineers not only love bagging peaks, but are also somewhat obsessed with maps, specifically topographic renderings. The ability to depict something massive, beautiful, and three-dimensional in a one-dimensional drawing is truly an art. Looking at topos of Grays and Torreys Peaks (named in honor of botanists Asa Gray and John Torrey), it's easy to see why these two peaks are usually done in tandem. Even though these 14ers are well-traveled, it's still important to study and know the geographical traits of the mountain before attempting a summit. Studying prominent points, such as the face of nearby Kelso Mountain, the rock pinnacle known as Rascal, and the big drop down into Lost Rat Couloir, can help guide you and add to your hiking experience. Identifying possible water sources and places to camp are equally important tasks. Turning the flat picture map in front of you into the hulking summit you are seeking helps you mentally plan and prepare for the climb ahead. Even so, you have to know how to read a map to make it come to life. Visualize what the contour lines represent—those pressed and squeezed close together distinguish steepness, while those stretched far apart indicate gentle slopes. Imagine yourself in the map and on the path to turn a one-dimensional shape into the amazing three-dimensional summit that is your goal.

But the Helper, the Holy Spirit,
whom the Father will send in My name,
He will teach you all things,
and bring to your remembrance all that I said to you.
John 14:26

I love that God is a trinity. We have Father, Son, and Holy Spirit to make our faith become three-dimensional. Although I still have a lot to understand about this mystery of the Trinity, pondering it helps bring my faith to life. First, there is Jehovah, the one true God who sits in Heaven. He is the Creator, the Master, the Lord of My Life. We get to experience Jehovah in His word, through the stories of other men and women in the Old Testament. But to make Him seem a little more real and accessible to me, *personally*, God sent His son, Jesus, to walk the earth, experiencing first hand the same mountaintops and valleys—the same places that are pressed close together—so He can walk the same map I am walking and put Himself in my shoes. And then He died. Sometimes that is so hard for me to understand. But it is not the end of the story because we have the Resurrection. How great is the gift of the Holy Spirit, the Helper, sent to us on Jesus' behalf to give us greater understanding of His Word and how He is working within us! The precious gift of the Holy Spirit takes the one-dimensional and truly makes it come alive in three-dimension.

Dear Lord, we humbly put the map of our lives in the hands of the Trinity. Though we may not be able to see the trajectory or the topography, we keep faith knowing the Father, the Son, and the Holy Spirit are at work. We thank You for sending Your Son to walk the earth, and for Your continued presence in the precious gift of the Holy Spirit. In Jesus' Name, Amen.

Date of Hike:

Climbing Party:

Notes:

LONGS PEAK

   As foot traffic on Colorado's 14,000 foot peaks continues to rise, what to do about its impact on the mountains is the source of much debate. My family and friends have unintentionally contributed to this congestion. Our love of the mountains is hard to contain, and we have encouraged others to take up climbing 14ers as well. Various agencies have been researching ways to balance the preservation of the beautiful landscapes with the demand for people clamoring to climb. The thought of not being able to pick up at any time and hike any mountain I choose is a bit disconcerting, but I understand the conundrum. In order to lessen hiker impact, some researchers propose a lottery system or pushing back trail heads to make hikes longer, harder, and therefore less desirable. Most foot traffic happens on the Front Range, thus keeping the other mountains more pristine. Those peaks, being so close to metro Denver, already bear the brunt of thousands of people wanting to summit. For the sake of the other 14,000 foot peaks, we might have to offer up Longs Peak and Mount Evans as a sacrifice to preserve the many other magnificent trails. Sacrifice means the act of offering something precious or the destruction of one thing for the sake of something else. We might have to sacrifice certain peaks in order to restore life to some of the trampled peaks we are "loving to death."

> *Don't imagine us leaders to be something we aren't.*
> *We are servants of Christ, not his masters.*
> *We are guides into God's most sublime secrets,*
> *not security guards posted to protect them.*
> *1 Corinthians 4:1 (the Message)*

Climbing a 14er is no easy feat. It takes a lot of training, preparation, and a certain mindset to continue on far above the treeline. Those of us who have attempted and succeeded might be tempted to consider ourselves part of an elite club, privileged to see the world from a vantage point few will ever witness. Does our pride in our accomplishment deter or encourage others to follow in our path?

Can the same be said about our Christian faith? When we accept Christ as our Savior, do we consider ourselves part of an elite crowd, better than others because we have seen the world from a vantage point that others may never see or understand? Do we pride ourselves for living above the line? Does our pride in our faith deter or encourage others to follow the path? Scripture is clear here that we are to be *servants* of Christ, and we are entrusted to share Him with the world. We are not gatekeepers. We are stewards. Let us remember this and share the mysteries of the Lord, serving as guides helping people stay on the path.

Dear Lord, up in the mountains and the high country, we feel closer to You. We give up a warm bed, hot meals, and ease of life to strike out in the wilderness. We rise up in altitude and work on conquering our fears and limitations. These are such meager sacrifices when we compare them to the sacrifices You made for all of us. In Your life on earth, You were all about sacrifice. There is so much beauty in sacrifice. You knew You could bear these burdens to ensure our eternal life. We are eternally grateful for that. In Jesus' Name, Amen.

Date of Hike:

Climbing Party:

Notes:

PIKE'S PEAK

••

Pike's Peak—it's the mountain that inspired Katharine Lee Bates to write the opening lines to her song, "America, the Beautiful." Looking out over the Rocky Mountains and the vast Eastern Colorado prairie could inspire anyone to start writing songs, poems, or books. A treasured song written while standing on Pike's Peak is hard to top when it comes to mountain lore. Pike's Peak is the easternmost 14er in the United States and has the highest elevation gain in Colorado, rising over 7,600 feet. Easily accessible from Colorado Springs, Pike's Peak is a popular 14er destination, but proximity does not equal easy climbing. The most common trail is the Barr Trail, located near Manitou Springs at 6,700 feet elevation, and it is a long twenty-four mile round trip. No matter which route you choose, the peak is a hard climb (unless you count riding in a car on the paved road to the top as a climb). To cut down on the sheer mileage, our family has made plans for someone to drive to the top and pick up fellow hikers. We avoid the long downhill and cut the trek in half. Regardless of the mileage, it's an amazing hike worth attempting—the views across the plains are hard to beat and the photo ops are unbelievable. It really is an American treasure.

I lift up my eyes to the mountains...
where does my help come from?
My help comes from the LORD, the Maker of heaven and earth.
Psalm 121:1 (NIV)

14

Someone once asked me if I experienced God more in the mountains or in the ocean. Since I am not a big fan of the beach—I can't sit still long enough to enjoy it—I was quick to answer the mountains. Whenever I drive into Colorado along Interstate 70 from Kansas, I become mesmerized as soon as I see the peaks in the distance. The sheer magnitude makes me feel so tiny in comparison. That is when I feel it—God's presence. I feel the solidness of the rock beneath my feet, and I look up. Some days I can barely make out the top of the mountain as it seems to reach directly up into Heaven. I think to myself how magnificent it is that the maker of the mountains is also my maker. No matter how small or insignificant I feel, He is there to help me...yes, *me*! It's no wonder that it inspired a song.

Dear Lord, thank You for beautiful skies, golden grain fields, and, best of all, purple-hued mountains. Your hand is seen entirely and exclusively. We could not imagine creating these wonders, but we are so glad You did. You are the magnificent Maker of all and we are so very grateful. In Jesus' Name, Amen.

Date of Hike:

Climbing Party:

Notes:

TORREYS PEAK

• •

Call it the "pick-a-rock" method of getting where you want to go. Climbing one 14er is hard enough, but to traverse a saddle and summit another mountain on the same day was almost more than I could comprehend. After making it to the top of Grays Peak in the Front Range, we turned westward to head down and back up to check Torreys Peak off the list. My two sons and husband bounded down the side of Grays and started the next ascent with vigor. I wanted to sit down on a rock and wait for them. I also wanted to cry. I was drained, but knew I would be disappointed if I came this far and didn't finish. So I picked a rock about ten feet away and told myself, "I can make it to that rock. Not sure I can go past there, but I can definitely make it to that rock." And I did. I picked another rock, put blinders on and completely focused on it. Again, I made it. And so on, up to the top of Torreys Peak and my waiting family. It was a huge mental and physical victory. I have used this approach in life many times since that day. By dividing the big tasks into smaller "rock" segments, those tough and seemingly unreachable goals somehow become reality.

The steps of a man are established by the LORD,
And He delights in his way. When he falls,
he will not be hurled headlong,
Because the LORD is the One who holds his hand.
Psalm 37:23-24

Throughout difficult seasons in my life, I find myself asking, "Who is my rock? Who am I putting my faith in to help me on my journey?" I find myself focusing on these questions when the climb gets tough. My rock can't be my spouse or my kids because, as this climb illustrated to me, we may not always be together or hiking at the same pace. No, my rock must be the Lord. He must be who I walk towards to sustain me.

When your rock is the Lord, Jehovah, you can rest in the truth that He has established all of your steps. He *delights* in the journey He takes with you, yes, even when the journey is difficult. And when you fall, which at some point you most certainly will, He will not cast you aside because He is sustaining you with His strength and power. It is with God as our rock that we achieve victory.

> *Father, thank You for being the rock that I walk towards. Thank You for establishing my steps and holding me up so that when I stumble I will not be hurled to the ground but will get up again through Your power and strength. In Jesus' Name, Amen.*

Date of Hike:

Climbing Party:

Notes:

Date of hike:

Climbing Party:

Notes:

MOSQUITO RANGE
AND TENMILE RANGE

MOUNT BROSS

It's amazing how the brain can change memories. With regards to hiking and mountain climbing, the brain alters memories, filtering the blood, sweat, and tears from a summit quest, leaving you with only the awesome reminders of success and invigoration. This is God's design, so that we keep trying difficult, uncomfortable tasks and continue to push and better ourselves. It's definitely one of the reasons many people keep hearing the mountains call to them. They are looking for that familiar exhilaration that comes with summiting.

Over the course of four decades, our family has figured out that it is best not to make any future hiking decisions as you are trudging towards a summit—or anytime right before or directly after a huge hike. Putting some time and distance between you and the mountains can help with perspective, but it can also develop into inaccurate memories. This was never more evident for us than on Mount Bross. It was a grueling hike that not only included our younger son getting sick on the top of the peak, but other factors that make our minds want to forget that day as well. But the fact that there was adversity cements its place as one of the most memorable. The group overcame opposition: weather, fatigue, illness, altitude, and burning lungs, to not only persevere, but to succeed. Now that the memories of hardship have faded, we are left with good feelings for the experience.

Blessed is a man who perseveres under trial;
for once he has been approved,
he will receive the crown of life which the Lord
has promised to those who love him.
James 1:12

When I am going through trials, the last thing I want to hear about is perseverance. More times than not, I am ready to toss in the towel and give up. But if I give up, then what? Those are the times I give it up to God. I ask Him why I am experiencing this trial and to please carry me through because I can't even seem to put one foot in front of the other to keep moving forward. And He does. Every time. And undoubtedly, after the trial passes, I look back with amazement that I came through it. I not only survived, but I am stronger, ready for the next trial that comes my way. As the verse promises, it is as if a wreath of victory has been placed on my head—even when it was God who carried me through.

Father, whatever trial I am going through today, large or small, let me give it to You. On my own, I am tempted to give up, to succumb, to wear out. But with You, I am strengthened and can persevere. Help me to give it all to You. In Jesus' Name, Amen.

Date of Hike:

Climbing Party:

Notes:

MOUNT DEMOCRAT

A few years back, I injured my elbow trying to start a temperamental lawnmower coupled with lots of push-ups in a workout. Fortunately, the pain didn't keep us off the mountains, although it did challenge my hiking pole use. During a physical therapy session that followed, the therapist asked about my immediate fitness goals, as well as my goals for five and ten years down the road. The answer was simple—I want to keep up with my new granddaughter and do whatever she wants. I'm hoping that includes hiking mountains and more specifically, peaks over 14,000 feet. It's going to take a persevering will to meet those expectations. Realistically, that will involve a fairly serious devotion to fitness for the next fifteen to twenty years. At my current athletic level and age, the first hour of a 14er hike is so hard that I almost always want to quit. Months of training and the right attitude are needed for me to just keep putting one foot in front of the other. Discouragement can set in and settle. My husband always says, "You can't judge a hike by the first hour." He is right. But the attention to each step and keeping on the path is difficult and exhausting. One of the most rewarding aspects of summiting peaks has been doing it alongside family, including parents, children, siblings, cousins, nieces, and nephews. It would be amazing to add grandchild to that list. There's nothing more satisfying than accomplishing a shared physical goal with someone you love. Many fond family memories have been made on the slopes of

Colorado peaks—a screensaver picture of my husband and two sons atop Mount Democrat comes to mind. It would be awesome to stand on the summit of any peak, no matter how high, with a grandchild and make another intergenerational milestone memory.

Devote yourselves to prayer,
keeping alert in it with an attitude of thanksgiving.
Colossians 4:2

We live in a society of instant gratification and immediate response. If we want something, we can click on the Amazon app and order it from our phone within minutes. Similarly, we can send a text to a friend and expect to hear back from her in seconds. We begin to expect our thoughts to become actions before we've even had a good chance to mull them over in our minds. Expectations for immediate results transcend to all parts of our lives. Have you ever started a diet and become disappointed that the needle on the scale hadn't budged after twenty-four hours? Have you ever had anxiety because a friend didn't return an email within hours of reading it? Worst of all, have you ever felt rejected by God because your prayers didn't bring the results you were looking for on *your* timeline?

Scripture tells us to devote ourselves to prayer. In the original Greek text, devote means to be constant, to persevere. Prayer involves a persevering will, traveling over the long haul, despite opposition or disappointment. Furthermore, scripture also tells us to keep alert. Don't get lazy when you don't see immediate results but be grateful along the journey.

We may not see the answers to all of our prayers in our lifetime, but that doesn't mean they are not on God's timeline. They may be answered in the lives of our children or grandchildren so we must keep training—and persevering—for their sake.

Father, I want an attitude of prayer so that I may be in constant relationship with You. Help my impatient heart not grow weary when I don't see immediate answers to the longings of my heart. Instead, open my eyes to the little miracles and answers that surround me every day. Help me to notice each of them. Give me an attitude of gratitude. In Jesus' Name, Amen.

Date of Hike:

Climbing Party:

Notes:

MOUNT LINCOLN

Mountain climbing is hard work. Since it's not typically our vocation, it doesn't have the same feel as our usual 9 to 5 job. The physicality and perspiration alone make it so different from many people's occupations. There's something about working up a good sweat that is so cathartic and cleansing. It's crazy how something kind of smelly and gross can make you feel clean and rejuvenated. Hiking in the mountains can cause an incredible cycle of sweat. You have bursts of hard work coupled with rest breaks that cool you off where your sweat dries rather quickly. This repetition of sweating and drying continues throughout the entire hike as you exert and rest, and in my opinion there are few things that smell worse than dried sweat. Back in our early years of hiking, we usually tent-camped. But these days, a shower at the end of the day can be a 14er trek deal breaker. Interestingly, the more fit you are, the sooner you start to sweat and from there your sweat volume only continues to increase. While this seems counterintuitive, it's true. When you start a hard workout or a hike and you've properly trained, the sweat will come fast and copious. Unfortunately, my body can't tell when I'm starting a workout or just running into work to drop something off—either way the sweat starts pouring. In the high country, the beginning of the hike can be quite warm in the lower elevations and sweating is a welcome relief. You can feel your body and spirit being cleansed by the exertion. Even though it's hard work, it feels like a sabbatical from our daily work.

*Six days you shall labor and do all your work,
but the seventh day is a sabbath of the LORD your God.
Exodus 20:9-10*

God created us for work. He is a God of work, creating the world and all of its unique creatures and animals and flora and fauna and bugs and humans and—well, you know the story. He created *everything*. But on the seventh day, He rested. Can't you just picture God, sitting back on a billowy cloud in Heaven, taking delight in all of His hard work? Isn't that what He wants us to do as well? Too often, we toil with blood, sweat, and tears at our daily jobs, paid or unpaid. We don't take time to sit back and reflect on the fruits of our labor. But God calls us to take a Sabbath day, to cease and desist from our usual work and reflect on what we have done, on what God did, and worship Him. How do you take your Sabbath? For me, there is nothing like a good hike—or being out in nature—to change my perspective on life. Being in His creation, I realize how small I am and how big God is.

Dear Lord, let all we do in work be done for You. Let all we do on our rest day be for You as well. We will continually lift You up as we toil and labor in the glorious work You have destined for us. And when our work is done here on earth, we look forward to our blissfully happy, heavenly rest. In Jesus' Name, Amen.

Date of Hike:

Climbing Party:

Notes:

MOUNT SHERMAN

Your first 14er will always be special and something to remember. My first was almost my last. Mount Sherman, in the Mosquito Range, seemed like a good choice—straightforward route, no scrambling, and just a little over 14,000 feet. But barely a quarter-mile up the trail, I felt like I was in real trouble. Even with training and acclimating properly, I was light-headed, sick to my stomach, and huffing and puffing. And praying fiercely. Being a rookie, I thought this must be normal, and I didn't want to let my husband/climbing partner down. At the time, I had no idea what was at the root of these symptoms—I just thought Colorado 14ers were probably not for me. My stubbornness kicked in and I summited with no intent of ever setting foot on a peak again. In a classic case of "you should listen to your body," a few days later, I found out I was five weeks pregnant with our second child. We were overjoyed, but I was also very scared, as it is not recommended to go over 10,000 feet in elevation while expecting. The lofty experience had a wonderful outcome. Fast forward twenty-six years, and our son has developed a love of hiking, and soars high as a proud member of the US Air Force.

In the same way, the Spirit also helps our weakness;
for we do not know how to pray as we should,
but the Spirit himself intercedes for us with
groanings too deep for words.
Romans 8:26

Last week I sat with a friend who has been walking through some difficult stuff for the past few years. I do this a lot with different friends as I've been told I am a good listener. But in this particular situation, I had run out of words to say to her. I couldn't even think of what to pray because honestly, we didn't know what the best outcome would be. We knew that we couldn't possibly understand what was going on and why it had gone on for so long. Our hearts were heavy. Isn't that the way it is a lot of times—our hearts are heavy, and we don't know why? We aren't feeling quite like ourselves, but we have no explanation. Sometimes we are going through so much that we don't even have the words to know what to ask for in prayer. That is when I turn to this verse. I take comfort in the fact that, in those situations, the Holy Spirit's got my back. I can just groan in pain and He takes those groans—not even words because I am *out* of words—and lifts them up in prayer to the Father. Somehow, just knowing that lifts my burden as I sense Him coming alongside of me in my weakness and infirmity. He knows what we need, even if we don't. That is the greatest comfort of all.

Father, You know our hearts and minds even better than we do. When all we can do is groan, we know You hear our groans and understand the depth of our heartache. We are thankful that You are always with us, and in times of weakness, You are our strength. In Jesus' Name, Amen.

Date of Hike:

Climbing Party:

Notes:

QUANDARY PEAK

Quandary Peak, the highest summit in the Tenmile Range of the Rockies, is near Breckenridge and therefore tends to be heavy in foot traffic. It's categorized as an "easy" summit. But make no mistake—there are no "easy" 14ers, just mountains of varying degrees of difficulty. The toughness of this summit came to light for me when visiting with a friend who does marathons. She declared that climbing Quandary Peak was harder than running a marathon. This comparison shocked me, as running has never been my forte. It highlighted the fact that

14,000 foot peaks can be very hard. This peak is also billed as "accessible year-round." A failed winter climb by my husband and his friend would attest to otherwise. The gentleness of the ascent may indicate less danger of avalanches, however, slabs of snow with cracks high up on the mountain were enough to send the climbing party back down and away from snow danger. There was no summit to be had that cold day.

Trust in the LORD with all your heart
And do not lean on your own understanding.
Proverbs 3:5-6

It often feels like we are climbing Quandary Peak daily. Events may occur that leave us confused because of our perspective. Situations may be more difficult than we ever imagined. Outcomes may not be what we envisioned. In other words, life is not going as we had planned. That is when we find ourselves asking the questions, "Why is this so hard? Why is this happening? I am doing all the right things—why is life so hard? Why does it feel like I can't make it?"

We are often left bewildered, perplexed, confused, essentially in a state of quandary. There are some things we can't possibly understand or make sense of on our own. In those times, we need to have confidence in the Lord with all of our hearts to make sense of the senseless, feeling secure in the fact that He is ultimately in control.

Father, help us to always trust in You. It is easy to trust when things are going our way, when we understand. But we ask for Your help in trusting You when things don't make sense. Help us to lean on the promise that You are in control and not us. In Jesus' Name, Amen.

Date of Hike:

Climbing Party:

Notes:

SAWATCH RANGE

MOUNT ANTERO

One of the most special 14er summits in our family lore involves Mount Antero, where three generations reached the top together. On a truly amazing day, my husband, his father, and our son made the trek up the mountain. Mount Antero, located in the Sawatch Mountain Range, is known among gem enthusiasts as a place to find aquamarine, topaz, and quartz crystals. On a crystal clear day without a cloud in the sky, known in mountaineering circles as a "bluebird" day, an 8-year-old, a 32-year-old, and a 59-year-old stood on the summit together for a treasured moment. Located in the San Isabel Forest near Buena Vista, the mountain is the tenth highest in Colorado and gets lots of traffic in the summer. A four-wheel drive road can get hikers up to 13,700 feet, making it easily accessible and, therefore, a busy peak in every season. Expect lots of people trekking on this mountain beside you. Depending on what you are looking for, Mount Antero has a wide variety of experiences awaiting hikers—of any generation.

Do this because you are a people set apart
as holy to GOD, your God.
GOD, your God, chose you out of all the people on
Earth for himself, a cherished, personal treasure.
Deuteronomy 7:6 (the Message)

It's one thing to hear about the "Rocky Mountain High" of climbing a 14er, but until you actually make the trek yourself, you can not fully experience the joy—the treasure—of being on the summit and looking over God's kingdom. Although the number of hikers is rapidly growing, only a select few climb 14ers. An even smaller group actually make a "Grand Slam" and complete all fifty-four, an impressive accomplishment.

We all have things we treasure on Earth. These treasures may be people, possessions, even accomplishments. It's a good reminder to me to think about what those things are now and again. Are my treasures—my loves—in the right order or do they need a readjustment from time to time? I also often wonder whose treasure am *I*. In a world that is becoming increasingly disconnected, sometimes it is hard to know for certain. That is why I feel so reassured when I read that the *Lord* chose me. He cherishes *me* as His personal treasure, set apart as holy. What a statement, to know that I am, and you are, chosen by the Lord, as His.

Dear Lord, family is something to be cherished. We thank You for both our biological and friend families that we collect on our journey. We endeavor to share Your word with all of the people we encounter in our lives. Help us to find the word gems to share that lift You up and guide people towards the treasured kingdom of Heaven. In Jesus' Name, Amen.

Date of Hike:

Climbing Party:

Notes:

MOUNT BELFORD

• •

Once every summer and once every winter, my family would escape western Kansas and head to the glorious Colorado Rocky Mountains. We would search and scour the horizon as we drove west along Interstate 70. It was always a game to see who could spot the mountains first. Little did I know that someday I would be scaling those majestic peaks. After navigating through Denver, our car would struggle as we headed up in altitude. Then, there was a payoff to the long car ride—a nondescript concrete overpass. It doesn't seem noteworthy, but it's an absolute engineering marvel. It perfectly frames the high country, and provides a glimpse of the beautiful Rockies in all their glory. Even if you are the driver, you can still see the view through the rectangular bridge "lens" and get a sense of the awe-inspiring vistas ahead. It's near a very steep portion of the interstate that features white-knuckle-driving with gradients of up to seven percent. Because of this, there are seven runaway truck ramps that are ingeniously engineered to safely stop a vehicle with failing brakes. Runaway ramps are gravel-filled extra lanes that parallel the main road and allow vehicles to exit and gradually stop using an incline. But the man-made marvels don't hold a candle to the natural ones. There is so much to see along the main artery through the state. The "lens" offers a little taste of what lies ahead, off the beaten path: a quick glance into all the beauty and majesty that the mountains behold.

41

For I consider that the sufferings of this
present time are not worthy
to be compared with the glory that is to be revealed to us.
Romans 8:18

Some days and seasons seem to follow a straight and narrow path. There aren't too many ups or too many downs. It's easy and predictable and sometimes even boring. Other days I wake up on top of the world, full of the Spirit and my heart filled with song. Then something happens—a phone call, a text, or a stinging comment—and I seem to make a sharp turn. Something changes and it all heads downhill. Often it happens so fast that I feel like a truck out of control. I want to take the exit for a runaway ramp in order to get off the road I am on. But I don't. I hold on and literally pray for Jesus to get in the driver's seat. The older I get the more I find myself getting anxious. I don't like speed. I don't like to feel out of control. But I hang on, growing more confident of who *is* in control. Each time, without fail, I make it through that downhill path only to catch another glimpse of God's glory as He reveals Himself to me on the journey.

Father, help me to see that the sufferings of
this world are only temporary. I can let myself
get all worked up over a comment—or lack of—
and let that spin into negative thought patterns
that consume my time and make me anxious.
Instead, help me to keep these thoughts in
proper perspective so that my mind can be
focused on the eternal glory that lies before
me. In Jesus' Name, Amen.

Date of Hike:

Climbing Party:

Notes:

MOUNT COLUMBIA

•••

It's so important to choose your climbing partners wisely. Over the years, my husband and I have had "tryouts" for hikers and campers. Most were a great success, but there were a few clunkers. It takes a certain mix of people to make a good climbing group, work group, or basic traveling group for that matter. It's imperative to have a person who is comfortable in a leadership position, someone who has commanding authority combined with the knowledge needed for pacesetting and getting the group up the mountain. This person must also bend and be flexible when circumstances arise, and humble themselves, recognizing the needs of the group. An individual who can guide with steadiness and continuity can be the key to mountaineering success. However, the summit isn't the end of the journey, the group must get down. Unfortunately, there have been instances where climbing parties have clashed, leading to tragic outcomes. This typically happens on the down-climb where factors, such as dangerous terrain and differing opinions on mountaineering techniques like route-finding, lead to a group separation. In fact, 75 percent of falls on mountains occur on the descent. A mixture of exhaustion, uneven ground, and letting your guard down after reaching your goal can combine to make the descent more treacherous. When looking for compatible climbing companions, it's important to meet beforehand to set goals, level expectations, and develop back-up plans, including weather flexibility. Making sure everyone is on the same page will set you up for the best chance at summit success and is integral for a happy and cohesive group.

He leads the humble in justice,
And He teaches the humble His way.
Psalm 25:9

My older sister loved the outdoors, especially the mountains, and she constantly tried to goad me into hiking. The problem was we were not compatible hikers: she was overly bossy and I was relentlessly stubborn. The more she told me I wasn't moving fast enough or working hard enough, the more I dawdled. I did not like being told what to do by anyone, but especially by her. She passed away from cancer five years ago, and as I processed through my grief and our complicated relationship, I ironically began to take up hiking.

Through that missed opportunity, I have learned the significance of humility, both in life and on the trail. If you continually shrug away from authority, it makes the journey much more difficult, not to mention less enjoyable, and you often end up missing the view. When I started hiking, I had to shed myself of excess pride on the trails because the mountains immediately humbled me. They zapped my oxygen levels. They depleted my energy. They taxed my legs. Literally, they broke my spirit and exhausted me. Next to the mountains, I felt so small. No matter how much I trained or how sophisticated my equipment was, I could not "best" the mountains. Try as I might, I just didn't—and don't—have the physicality to complete a 14er. Only when I stopped fighting it was I able to hike other trails and catch a glimpse of what my sister had been trying to share with me. If only we both had been a little bit more like Jesus—if she had been gentler and I had been less prideful—we might have been able to reach the summit together.

Dear Heavenly Father, help me to humble my heart. Help me to not be so stubborn that I miss the ways that You want to show me. When I am humbled, give me a heart to understand what You are trying to teach me, instead of a heart that focuses on always wanting to be in the lead. And Father, forgive me for those missed opportunities. In Jesus' Name, Amen.

Date of Hike:

Climbing Party:

Notes:

MOUNT ELBERT

Be prepared. It's the official Boy Scout slogan and a good rule of thumb, especially when climbing 14,000 foot peaks. Our family hiking motto expands on that premise: be prepared to spend the night on the mountain. It has served us well over the years. It makes your backpack much heavier and can slow you down a little, but it's worth the peace of mind knowing that we always have enough water, food, and clothing to wait out a weather event, an injury, or to assist another climber. Some hikers go with a "travel light" philosophy. Nine times out of ten, nothing goes wrong and unencumbered climbing is successful. But what about that one unexpected event? It's amazing what has come in handy over the years. That space blanket, which is essentially a long roll of tin foil, was actually pulled out and utilized once. The ever-present whistle was used to help Search and Rescue locate stranded hikers. The compass, Swiss army knife, mole skin, duct tape, extra headlamp batteries, water purification tabs were all needed and used at some point in the backcountry. On Mount Elbert, we shared extra water with a church group who had not adhered to another rule of thumb— carry at least one liter per person per 1,000 feet of elevation gain. Arm yourself with the essentials, and don't forget to put on the armor of God as well.

Be prepared, and prepare yourself, you and all your companies, that are assembled about you, and be a good guard for them.
Ezekiel 38:7

Preparedness. The Lord can't emphasize enough our need for it. He uses the word prepare (from the Hebrew word "kuwn," meaning firm, stable, to provide or furnish) twice in the first five words of this verse. Although this verse is talking about preparation for battle, it is similar to hiking. We are to prepare ourselves for all we need by gathering all of the supplies that we might need to sustain us. As we prepare to hike, don't we often carry a checklist of the supplies we might need in the event of an emergency? Supplies like water, matches, emergency blanket, and backup batteries frequently end up on this list.

In this scripture, God says we need to prepare *ourselves* as well. How do we do that? We need to continually seek Him, fixing our eyes on Him as the sustainer and provider of all of our needs. By seeking Him through scripture reading, praying, worshiping, and serving others, we are preparing ourselves for whatever situation we might find ourselves in.

Father, help me to be prepared for whatever the day brings. Help me to always seek You first, in all situations, as I know that You will provide all that I need to protect me. Prepare my family as well, serving as a protector for whatever unforeseen circumstances they might confront in the days ahead. In Jesus' name, Amen.

Date of Hike:

Climbing Party:

Notes:

MOUNT HARVARD

• •

When our family was first becoming hikers and climbers in the late '80s, we spent a lot of time learning various techniques for safety and first aid. My husband always says, "The best rescue in the wilderness is a self-rescue." Search and Rescue operations have greatly expanded since those days—thankfully, I might add, as we've had to use a SAR group ourselves. But I still remember my husband practicing his stitching techniques, on pig's feet he got from the grocery store butcher, in case of a deep laceration. In addition, we both keep our CPR certification current, which includes a First Aid section (there are several good backcountry first aid books on the market). Fortunately, with the advent of satellite phones and greater cell coverage, help is closer than ever before. Regardless, being prepared to get yourself off a mountain or administer quick, temporary aid to a victim until medical attention is available is invaluable. Another safety tip: study ground-to-air distress signals in the event phone communication is not an option. Using bright colored sleeping bags/pads/clothes, you can make a large "V" for "need assistance" or an "X" for "need medical attention" to alert nearby aircraft to your situation. Be ready to use a mirror as well, to confirm location when you see a helicopter or plane in the area. Hopefully, none of these tips will be needed, but it's a good idea to be familiar with basic first aid and distress signals in case rescue is needed.

I have called upon You, for You will answer me, O God;
Incline Your ear to me, hear my speech.
Psalm 17:6

I teach a life skills and communications class inside of the walls of a community corrections facility. One of the techniques I teach my students and model in conversations with them is called SOLER, which was developed by Gerard Egan. It is a method of demonstrating that you are being attentive to a conversation.

S—Squarely face the person
O—Open posture
L—Lean in
E—Eye contact
R—Relaxed demeanor

Lean in. That's exactly what this scripture says. If I call out to the Lord, He will *lean in* to listen to me, and He will answer me. He is, in essence, being attentive to me.

A few years ago, after going through a difficult time, I needed someone to really listen to me. I had gone to friends before and they had been there for me, but I was beginning to feel like I was becoming a burden. I imagined they were avoiding eye contact when they saw me coming (this was not really true, but it's how I felt). Counselors had their place as well, but I didn't feel like they really *heard* me. I thought I had a pretty good grip on my situation. I wasn't looking for an assessment of my troubles as much I longed for a way forward. I spent that summer calling out to the Lord. He listened through my tears on the porch. He listened to me process on long walks. That summer, I tangibly felt Him leaning in to hear me whisper. And He answered me. What a beautiful Maker we have who will incline—even bend down—to our level in order to hear our whispers and rescue us.

Father, how grateful I am to worship a god who inclines himself to me. My desire is to have a voice that is heard and to remember that You promise to listen and respond. Father, I cherish that You are leaning in to listen to me—it makes me want to lean in even closer to You. In Jesus' name, Amen.

Date of Hike:

Climbing Party:

Notes:

MOUNT OF THE HOLY CROSS

Mount of the Holy Cross is one of the peaks that helped inspire us to write a devotional book geared toward 14ers and those who climb them. Years ago, spectacular photos showed a near-perfect snow cross on the mountainside made from a prominent ridge and ravine. Erosion has been at work, but usually the faintest hint of a cross can be seen. Mount of the Holy Cross is a particularly rugged and long hike in the huge Holy Cross Wilderness. Although many hikers solo 14ers, it's generally a good rule of thumb to hike in groups. This creates a "checks and balances" system, which aids in avoiding bad decisions. Groups should hike at the speed of the slowest member. This may seem irritating at times, but it could be you the next day. Nevertheless, groups separate for various reasons, such as photo stops or fatigue. There have been numerous cases of hikers lost and separated from their climbing party. Sticking together truly saves time in the long run. In a wilderness as vast as Holy Cross (over 100,000 acres and 164 miles of trail), it's especially important to avoid getting separated. Always tell someone where you are going, when to expect your return—and what to do if you don't.

We urge you, brethren, admonish the unruly,
encourage the fainthearted, help the
weak, be patient with everyone.
1 Thessalonians 5:14

I realize organized religion is not for everyone. Some folks— maybe many hikers—feel like they can find God in the beauty of nature. I used to feel like that myself. Church was filled with people who knew all the right words and prayed all the right prayers. But they didn't really live out their faith beyond the walls of the church. I think I was mistaken. Now, I take comfort in my church. I see that everyone is moving toward a similar goal and that everyone has individual struggles, many of which we cannot see. I found that when I was "walking alone," I tended to wander off the trail. I believed I was following the right path, the true path, only to find myself not slightly off, but ultimately lost in the wilderness. I am thankful now that I am part of a supportive Christian community. I find that we are able to encourage each other and support one another along our journeys. I have words that encourage my friends, and likewise, they have words that encourage me. We may all be walking at a different pace, but a good faith community will be patient, making sure everyone makes it to the ultimate destination.

Dear Lord, as we navigate the wilderness, help us to show our gratitude for those around us. Our friends and family help us stay on the path to You and gently steer us when we wander off the route. We give the ultimate thanks to our supportive Christian community and are so fortunate to share our joys and sorrows with them. We are all in this together, keeping our eyes toward our ultimate destination. In Jesus' Name, Amen.

Date of Hike:

Climbing Party:

Notes:

HURON PEAK

Acclimating is such an important part of mountain climbing. Endless research shows the major role it plays in safe, and therefore successful, summiting. The consequences of not spending a few nights at higher altitude range from a mild headache to very dangerous, life-threatening conditions. Unless you already live at an elevation over 6,000 feet, it's important to properly acclimate. For those of us coming from flatlands to 14ers, we typically spend a couple nights in the mile high city of Denver before heading up higher for a few nights and set up for summit day. Of course, that is in an ideal world where time is limitless. In reality, we have often driven across Kansas, camped at the trailhead and then attempted a peak the next day, without success. In order to combat high altitude sickness, my husband takes medicine, and I've been fortunate not to suffer significantly. But I can sure tell the difference proper acclimating has on someone who lives at approximately 1,000 feet above sea level. For my husband, the climb up Huron Peak was dictated by work schedules and hiking partner timetables. That left him with very little flexibility to get to the peak and climb. Inflexibility certainly does not set one up for summiting success, but it does make one consider moving to Colorado.

And do not be conformed to this world,
but be transformed by the renewing of your mind,
so that you may prove what the will of God is,
that which is good and acceptable and perfect.
Romans 12:2

The Greek word for transform is metamorphoo, meaning to change into another form. When hiking in the mountains, we go through a physical transformation when we acclimate. Research shows that when we spend more time at higher elevations, we allow our bodies to adjust and form more hemoglobin, which carries more oxygen throughout our bodies.

It can be like that for our spiritual life as well. When we spend more time in prayer or in God's word, we allow our minds to be transformed and renewed so that we can test God's will for our lives. The more time we spend with God, reading His word and conversing in prayer, the more our hearts become transformed. As with acclimating before a hike, these spiritual disciplines do not guarantee that life will be easy or free of trouble. However, taking time to be with God allows us to see more clearly His will for our lives, which is good, acceptable, and perfect. This renewal through relationship with God gives us better conditions to endure the journey.

Dear Heavenly Father, I long to spend time in Your word every day, but oftentimes my to-do list exceeds my time, and quiet time with You gets pushed to the side. Help me to make You a priority each morning so that my thoughts and actions throughout the day are guided by the words You plant in my heart. In Jesus' Name, Amen.

Date of Hike:

Climbing Party:

Notes:

LA PLATA PEAK

Of the many guidelines of hiking 14ers, one is: stay on the trail. This can sometimes mean that you're not on the most direct route. While switchbacks can be frustrating and maddening, it is best for the mountain terrain and helps preserve the area for other hikers. A late mountain snow and sloppy, muddy conditions on La Plata Peak in the Sawatch Range caused us to get off route and follow a fellow hiker's footprints. This ultimately led to our small climbing group inadvertently trampling on fragile wildflowers. We did our best to correct the situation, but we still caused damage. Paths and borders are there for good reason. Many skiers have gotten in trouble in the backcountry when they've ignored ski boundary signs and ventured beyond the barriers. It's the same for wilderness boundaries and trails—they are there to keep climbers and campers as safe as possible. With the rise of GPS and aerial photography, you are more likely to stay on the right path. On a recent climb, my husband and his hiking cousin printed out step-by-step photographs to help them with accurate route-finding. Those pictures, along with less sophisticated piles of rocks (cairns), helped mark the paths and boundaries, making a successful summit within reach.

The lines have fallen to me in pleasant places,
Indeed, my heritage is beautiful to me.
Psalm 16:6

Boundary lines. I find them necessary, but why are they so hard to stay inside? When I was a teenager, my parents set very loose boundaries. I don't know if it was the era I grew up in, if it was because I was the last of four children, or if it was because my parents assumed I was a pretty good kid. Whatever the reason, my parents—especially my sweet, but naïve mother—didn't always set very strict rules. Now, I am a rule follower, so I tried to adhere to the ones I could clearly see. But if they were sketchy, I crossed the lines and headed into unsafe territory more times than I would like to admit. One time in particular, I had a feeling I *kind of* knew where the grey boundary line was, but I dared to cross it anyway. I found myself in a not so pleasant place where bad decisions could have easily set me on a course for disaster. Fortunately, my parents caught me before I got into too much trouble. I look back with gratitude that they quickly reset those boundary lines with more clarity—no more getting off track in the wilderness of bad temptations for this girl.

The lesson I learned from that particular night greatly

influenced my own parenting. When my girls were teens, I set clear boundaries for them. I did so not to be mean or punish them, but because I knew that I thrived more when I knew where the lines were. I assumed that would be true for them as well. As a result, those boundaries helped keep my daughters safe in an unsafe world. Of course, they tipped their toes across the line, but because they knew that I was watching carefully, they didn't find themselves figuratively "falling off a cliff."

Father, thank You for the boundary lines You set in our lives. You set them to help us flourish. When we venture outside the lines and find ourselves outside of Your will, You always welcome us back. Help us to realize the goodness in those boundaries and not trample outside of them. In Jesus' Name, Amen.

Date of Hike:

Climbing Party:

Notes:

MOUNT MASSIVE

●●

"Come on! Hurry up!" These words were frantically spoken by my husband's faithful hiking partner as they briefly sat on the summit of Mount Massive. My husband had stopped to put on his "gaiters," hiking armor that snaps around the lower part of the leg to keep snow, dust, rocks, or muck out of hiking boots. When the duo had approached the mountaintop, they came face-to-face with a nasty storm brewing on the other side of the ridge. They did not see the black, ominous clouds as they made their ascent. After the quickest of summit stops, the pair decided to descend as fast as possible. As they scurried down the mountain, they saw lightning bolts hitting the ground *below* their position. Hurrying as fast as safely possible, they were high-tailing it down the peak, when all of the sudden they felt an unfamiliar buzz. My husband describes it as "bees stinging your face." He looked over at his hiking partner and was startled to see his long, greasy hair standing on end. Then it hit. Simultaneous FLASH BOOM. The fillings in their teeth tingled and they crouched down as close to the ground as they could with minimal contact. Although there is no way to predict how close the lightning strike was, they estimate it was within 100 yards. The mere length of a football field separated the small hiking party from severe injury or worse on Mount Massive, the second highest peak in the Rocky Mountains.

Finally, be strong in the Lord and in his mighty power.
Put on the full armor of God, so that you can
take your stand against the devil's schemes.
Ephesians 6:10-11 (NIV)

Heading out the door for my morning walk, I realize I have some specific rituals that set me up for success. First, I put on my walking shoes. Next, I strap on my hippy pack (not very fashion conscious, but it keeps me hands free). Then I put on my baseball cap and sunscreen. Finally, I arm myself with pepper spray and water. As soon as I turn the door handle, my faithful companion Atticus flanks my side, ready to go. What I have learned through my training is that each of these pieces of equipment is critical to my success. Without any one of them, I leave myself vulnerable to injury, sunburn, dehydration, heat exhaustion, and, although I hate to imagine it, potential perpetrators.

Isn't it like that with the armor of God? Each piece that Paul tells us to put on protects us from being vulnerable to the dangers of the world. Leaving anything out exposes our weak spots to the enemy, leaving us vulnerable to attack. Putting on the armor ensures that the best partner, the Lord, is flanking me.

Putting on my gear for a walk has become second nature. Strapping on God's armor should be the same. Before I ever leave the house for the day, I should put on the armor of God, knowing it will protect me from the dangers I face as I walk into the world.

Father, as I enter this new day, let me put on the full armor of God to protect me from any unforeseen circumstances that might come my way. As I walk into whatever awaits me, let me walk in Your strength, knowing that You are protecting me from evil. In Jesus' Name, Amen.

Date of Hike:

Climbing Party:

Notes:

MISSOURI MOUNTAIN

Solitude is hard to find on many Colorado 14ers. Summer weekends find thousands of people on the peaks. It's tough to strike your hiking rhythm when the trail is at capacity. Over the years, we have fine-tuned our trip scheduling in order to encounter the least amount of people. For the most part, we do this to maximize the potential for quiet and solitude, but fewer people also means better parking at the trailhead. For less trail congestion, we try to hike during the week and pick peaks that are further from Denver. Whenever possible, we schedule hikes slightly into the offseason. This can be difficult to do at times because we must consider weather. We mandate ridiculously early starts for our parties in the hopes that we can have the summit to ourselves. The more difficult routes have fewer hikers, but those of us who prefer the less technical routes have to learn to hike in the multitudes. In order to avoid the masses, some mountaineers have even moved from climbing 14ers to the much less popular and traversed 13,000 foot peaks. One of our favorite ascents over the last thirty-five years of hiking in Colorado was Missouri Mountain. It offered hushed and peaceful solitude to enjoy the beautiful trek. Missouri Mountain was named by the miners who came from the Show-Me state to make their riches. Today, its riches are mainly enjoyed by hikers who venture here.

"Come to me, all you who are weary and
heavy-laden, and I will give you rest.
Take my yoke upon you and learn from Me,
for I am gentle and humble in heart,
and YOU WILL FIND REST FOR YOUR SOUL.
For My yoke is easy and My burden is light."
Matthew 11:28-30

As I was heading out the door for a training walk, my daughter texted me and asked what I listen to on my walks. I pondered this question while out on the trail. My first week of walking consisted of Christian music and sermons. Early in the second week, I switched to podcasts and a little John Denver to get me in the Colorado spirit. By the end of the last week, as I was doing my "long" walk for the week on a pretty isolated trail, I decided to ditch my headphones and just listen to what was going on around me. At first, all I could hear was my heavy breathing and the slight click in my knee as I made each step. But the further I got on the trail, the more I noticed the sounds of the Creator, as though He were speaking to me. I heard the chorus of crickets cheering me on. I saw a cardinal, which always reminds me of my earthly father, intermittently cross my path as if to show me the way. And I heard God speaking to me through the songs and scriptures that kept playing in my head. I realized that this time without headphones is sacred space. It is just me and my Maker on this trail, yoked together. When I don't fight Him, the yoke is easy. And as we walk together, He is whispering sweetly in my ear, giving rest to my soul.

Dear Lord, thank You for solitude and for helping eliminate distractions as we pray to You. Your Son on earth exemplified this as he prioritized seclusion in prayer. Help us to look upon these times of isolation, wherever they may be, as a wonderful way to get closer to You. In Jesus' Name, Amen.

Date of Hike:

Climbing Party:

Notes:

MOUNT OXFORD

Driving up to Independence Pass from Leadville to Aspen, we couldn't believe the amount of avalanche debris. Every few miles, the eerie beauty of downed trees in big swaths caught our attention. The debris paths were a mile wide and contained such force that after crushing one side of the mountain they crossed the road, rushing uphill to knock down more old-growth trees on the other side. The unprecedented avalanche onslaught was due to the winter of 2018-2019 that brought historic snowfall to the Colorado high country. Aspen received

396 inches of snow, and even lower cities like Buena Vista near Mount Oxford netted over seventy-five inches. Early season snow coupled with massive blizzards in the spring made for perfect avalanche conditions. Unfortunately, because of the avalanches, there was loss of life in Colorado that season. My husband and I thought of our friend who died in an avalanche near Lake Louise in Banff National Park, Alberta, Canada. He left his wife and two young daughters at the hotel while he went out for an early morning hike. It's a stark reminder to always take a conservative approach when dealing with avalanche prone areas.

A time to give birth and a time to die;
A time to plant and a time to uproot what is planted.
Ecclesiastes 3:2

This scripture has often surfaced during the many funerals I have attended in my lifetime. With the lilting melody, it has given me hope in times of sorrow. It wasn't until just recently that the second part of this verse really got my attention. I have moved ten times in my lifetime, and I identified with this verse whenever it was time to plant new roots. Now, however, the word "uproot" has taken on a new meaning. The Hebrew word for uproot is "aqar' which means to pluck up, root up, to cut or to hamstring. "To pluck" means to separate abruptly or forcibly, and "to hamstring" means to make ineffective or powerless. That image brings to mind the trees that are plowed down by snow during an avalanche. An avalanche's force is powerful and due to a shift below the surface that sometimes can't be seen.

Recently, I went through a very painful ending to a friendship. I did not see it coming. What felt like a friendship established on fun adventures, shared experiences, and prayer times ended abruptly in one day. The accusations and cutting words left me crippled for a long time. As I tried to sort through the debris and understand what I had done to offend, I realized that there was nothing left. No feelings, no apologies, no hope for reconciliation. Somehow there had been a shift so deep, yet I didn't even sense it coming. Perhaps, I was plucked out of that relationship for a reason...by the Lord. Perhaps, there had been warning signs all along. Perhaps, this was not a friendship established on healthy ground and could not withstand any pressure. I was plucked out of it for reasons only God knows. I have to trust in His plan, reassured that out of the debris will spring new growth.

Dear Lord, sometimes we don't recognize the slippery slope that we are on. Thank You for plucking us from these situations and keeping us on the path You have set for us. We defer to Your timeline with the understanding that where You plant us is the right place to be. In Jesus' Name, Amen.

Date of Hike:

Climbing Party:

Notes:

MOUNT PRINCETON

• •

As a senior, the tradition at our small western Kansas high school was a trip to Denver to tour various landmarks and expand our horizons. One of my classmates had never had the pleasure of making the four-hour car ride to the foothills of the Rockies. It was truly a blessing to see the awe on her face when we got within site of the Front Range. It's so hard to explain the grandeur of the mountains as they rise up from the Eastern plains of Colorado. The peaks can't be fully appreciated except in person, and setting foot on those peaks makes hikers cherish them even more. Mount Princeton is a good 14er to start that cycle of hiking delight. Although this Sawatch mountain is regarded as a conservative introduction to mountaineering, it is still a 14,000 foot mountain and must be respected as such. There is so much beauty on this hike, including the white chalk cliffs at the entrance of Chalk Creek Canyon. From those scenic cliffs, it's a rugged, husky climb, making the adage, "half your pace, double your fun," a great mantra. My husband's hiking party even encountered a couple in their 70s that exemplified that formula. From the top of that lofty peak, the snow melt travels six miles and 7,000 elevated feet down to drain into the Arkansas River. From there, it flows into the Mississippi River, the Gulf of Mexico, and eventually the Atlantic Ocean. It's an amazing plan, on a massive scale, and perfectly showcases God's grandeur in creation.

On the glorious splendor of Your majesty
And on your wonderful works, I will meditate.
Psalm 145:5

About six years ago, my daughter went to Frontier Ranch, a Young Life camp situated near the base of Mount Princeton in Buena Vista, Colorado. She spent the summer as a college staffer on the landscape team. My husband and I are pretty protective of our girls, so we didn't want her to make the ten-hour drive across Kansas and through the Rockies by herself. So he drove out with his 20-year-old girl, both of them belting out John Denver songs as soon as the mountains came into view. I picked her up six weeks later, a more mature 20-year-old who was singing a different tune. As soon as she got in my car, I could tell she was different. I spent the next ten hours on I-70 listening to her recall stories from her summer of all the things she had done, the new friends she had met, and most importantly, the change in her heart. She had been a Christian since she was small, but spending time in those mountains had taken her relationship with God to a new depth. She talked nonstop on that ride home. For me, it was like catching a glimpse into the window of her soul. I will never know everything that she experienced on that mountain, but I do know that camp changed her and that drive home is one of our most cherished car rides together.

Dear Heavenly Father, We praise You for
Your majesty. I long to spend my days meditating
on Your glorious works, letting Your goodness
be an overflow from my heart in my thoughts,
words, and deeds. In Jesus' Name, Amen.

Date of Hike:

Climbing Party:

Notes:

MOUNT SHAVANO

· ·

When catching a glimpse of Mount Shavano from the Arkansas River valley, we were fortunate to time it perfectly and actually spot the Angel of Shavano west of Salida. The angel is a snow formation that appears each spring as the mountain snow melts. The white-robed figure with outstretched arms on the slopes of the 14,231 foot peak beckons hikers to climb. The beauty of that climb? The standard route up puts you directly on the north wing of the angel. Don't we all want to be on the wing of an angel? There are many legends surrounding the Angel of Shavano. Most of them center around prayers for drought relief for the Sawatch Range and its surrounding valleys. It's clear from a quick Google search that many people have been inspired by this mountain and its angel. The heavenly configurations of the Angel of Shavano and the cross on Mount of the Holy Cross make these two peaks some of my favorites. The peak was named for Ute tribal Chief Shavano. Additionally, Tabeguache Peak, Mount Antero, and Mount Shavano are all derived from Ute words. Tabeguache and Shavano are often climbed together. They lie in the Sawatch Range, which derives its name from the Ute word "saguguachipa," meaning "blue earth." The blue-green forest on Mount Shavano provides a perfect frame to capture the contrast of the lily white Angel of Shavano.

For He will give His angels charge concerning you,
To guard you in all your ways.
Psalm 91:11

Who are the angels in your life? I used to envision angels as floating cherubs, sitting around on billowy clouds, strumming their harps. Now, I believe that angels are around me all the time, but I also believe that you have to look closely to see them. Like Shavano, they usually show up when I am melting... or having a melt down...or in a period of drought. When I am in crisis, suddenly an angel appears through the voice of a friend or the smile of a stranger. The angel might appear at just the right moment to offer a word of encouragement or to issue a word of warning. And as quickly as they appear, they might disappear as if they were never there at all. Only you know differently. The older I get the more I believe that those real life encounters with people confirm that God has His watchful eyes on me, guarding me at all times.

Dear Heavenly Father, thank You for those angels that have appeared throughout my life. Thank You for the times they have offered me a word of encouragement or a word of warning just when I needed it most. Please help me to always be on the lookout for the angels in my life, sent by You to remind me of Your watchful eye. In Jesus' Name, Amen.

Date of Hike:

Climbing Party:

Notes:

TABEGUACHE PEAK

Tabeguache Peak is in the Sawatch Range which runs through the heartland of Colorado. Fifteen of the state's 14ers are located in this range. For this reason, it makes sense to attempt more than one summit while in this area. This makes using rest days and knowledge of the mountaineering "rest step" even more valuable. A day of decompression, reflection, and replenishment is needed for everyone, and athletes are keenly aware of the importance of off days. When training for a 14er hike, or any endurance event, rest and rebuilding days should be scheduled in. Similar to how off days are needed for preparation, on the actual climb you need "rest steps," a hiking technique for energy conservation. When attempting Tabeguache Peak, a long, arduous hike that often has steep, firm snow, mastering the "rest step" can be beneficial. The rest step is essentially a pause in motion where the rear leg is vertically extended and the front leg is locked at the knee, but the quadricep is relaxed. This relieves the body of exertion as much as possible (YouTube videos are helpful to get the knack). You can take a breath, pause, and energize for the next step. Discipline is needed to master this gait, and all the while, the mountain is opposing you.

So there remains a Sabbath rest for the people of God.
For the one who has entered His rest has himself also
rested from his works, as God did from His.
Therefore, let us be diligent to enter that rest, so that no one
will fall, through following the same example of disobedience.
Hebrews 4:9-11

In the beginning, for six days, God worked hard, really hard, creating all of the world. And it was good work—He even says so. But on the seventh day, He rested. How often do our days get filled with *good* things that we are working on? We fill up our calendars so that we can justify having no time for rest. No time to pause for a Sabbath. Just writing those sentences shows me how arrogant I am. I find myself acting as if my work and my days are more important than God's. Are they so important that I can't pause to rest on the Sabbath? We need rest to reflect, refresh, and rebuild. Without rest, we risk injury to our body, our spirit and our soul. Resting takes discipline and diligence. Ironically, it takes work to get into the rhythm of rest. When we pause, we allow ourselves to rest, enjoy what we've accomplished, and ready ourselves for what's to come.

Dear Lord, in today's fast-paced world, it is
even more important than ever to take a break,
a rest, a Sabbath. Thank You for designing us
for work and then giving us an example of rest.
Let us use Your example of pausing for a day
to refresh ourselves. In Jesus' Name, Amen.

Date of Hike:

Climbing Party:

Notes:

MOUNT YALE

• •

We made the decision a few years ago to stop trying winter ascents of 14,000 foot peaks. Some people might thrive in those conditions, but we came to the realization that we really don't like being cold. Hiking when it's extremely hot isn't my favorite, but I will take it over freezing temps. On a February ascent in the Sawatch Range, one of the members of our climbing party got too close to the base of a tree and fell six feet down into a snow shaft, known as a tree well. It is an area of loose snow around the trunk of a tree surrounded by deep snow. Also called "spruce traps," these hollow openings are dangerous to hikers and anyone entering the backcountry in the winter. A tree's branches shelter its trunk from falling snow, where an area of very loosely-packed snow can form, allowing a trap to take shape. It's so deceptive because it looks just like the firmly-packed snow we had been walking on. Flailing and kicking only led our friend deeper into the fluffy powder. Freeing yourself from this pitfall can be difficult, if not impossible. In fact, avalanche institute research showed that 90 percent of people placed in tree wells were unable to rescue themselves. Luckily, my husband was able to assist our trapped friend and extricate him from the snowy depths. It was a scary situation and a great reminder of the many dangers that can be encountered in the backcountry.

My eyes are continually toward the LORD,
For He will pluck my feet out of the net.
Psalm 25:15

Have you ever gotten lost in your thoughts driving somewhere familiar? Before you know it, you have arrived, and you don't even know how you got there. I have. And if I am being honest, it kind of scares me. I become so accustomed to the familiar that I stop being aware of my surroundings and the warning signs that keep me safe. Luckily, in my driving, no mishaps have ever occurred. However, there are other situations in my life where I have ended up in a bad place because I wasn't paying attention. Once again, I was too comfortable in my familiarity to notice the warning signs. Perhaps, I strayed into a destructive relationship, developed unhealthy habits, or told myself little white lies to rationalize a behavior. Before too long, I became entangled in a mess that I wasn't sure how to escape. I am so thankful for my God and for His grace when I find myself trapped in these snares. When I remember to look up, His grace shows me the way out.

Dear Lord, encircle our hiking friends and those we meet on our daily walks in prayer, grace, and faith. When we are surrounded by fellow sojourners, the normal response is to look up. Therefore, we lift our eyes to You. We give You thanks for rescuing us out of snares and setting us on the right path. In Jesus' Name, Amen.

Date of Hike:

Climbing Party:

Notes:

SANGRE DE
CRISTO RANGE

BLANCA PEAK

It used to be so easy to round up a climbing group. Back in college, we would easily have seven or eight hikers commit to a 14er attempt. That was before jobs, family, and various other commitments. These days, we are lucky to find one or two game for the challenge. Big groups are fun to hike with, but sometimes it can feel like herding kittens. For three summers, our family led groups of forty to sixty high school cross country runners up a 12,000 foot peak on the western edge of Rocky Mountain National Park. That was a challenge. While we were blessed that everyone was in reasonably good physical shape, many of them had never attempted a serious hike and needed lots of coaching. They needed to know what to pack, trail etiquette, how to recognize the signs of altitude sickness, and even basics like bringing enough water. We took pride in getting all team members up the mountain every summer. There was so much joy when the students arrived at the summit. Slower hikers were given an encouraging celebration "tunnel" at the top of the peak. Instilling a love of hiking in these kids was a highlight of our summers. Years later, we still hear from alumni as they report their hiking successes. My husband even went so far as to take a small group up a 14er several years after they had been with us at a cross country camp. The bonds we formed with these kids on the slopes of a mountain continue to this day.

As soon as He was approaching, near the
descent of the Mount of Olives,
the whole crowd of the disciples began to praise God joyfully
with a loud voice for all of the miracles which they had seen.
Luke 19:37

Palm Sunday is one of my favorite Sundays in the life of the church. As a child, I was carried into the story personally when I got to wave a palm branch as I paraded with the other children through our church's sanctuary. Now I understand the story more deeply. While I still love the joyous parade, I know that after Palm Sunday we have to go through some pretty dark days before the Resurrection. I think about how quickly that crowd turned and wonder, "Would I have turned that quickly too?" The hard truth for me—and I would venture most of us—is yes.

This got me thinking of the crowd of people in my own life. Some have been joyfully cheering me on for years, while others abruptly shunned me for what seemed like no just cause. Some have helped me carry my burdens through some pretty tough times, while others have turned their backs when the going got tough. I am so grateful for those friendships that have stuck around.

I also wonder, "Who am I cheering on? Do I stick around at all times? Do I run away when things get tough?" I want to be the kind of friend who walks through life's ups and downs and who is constantly on the lookout for God's hand in all situations. I want to shout those miracles that I have witnessed with my friends, in their lives and in my own. I want to remind us all of the One who will never leave us, no matter the circumstance. I want to remember the One who is always there to cheer us on the path of righteousness. And I want to always have a heart and voice that speaks hope to my friends.

Dear Lord, we enthusiastically praise You in large crowds with loud booming voices. We also praise You in quiet moments with close friends. Thank You for those friends who stick with us during the ups and downs. You have blessed us with people in our lives who continually point us in Your direction. Help us to reciprocate and pass those blessings on to all. In Jesus' Name, Amen.

Date of Hike:

Climbing Party:

Notes:

CRESTONE NEEDLE

When preparing to climb a 14er, there are certain items you put into your pack to assure yourself of a successful climb. Some of the basics might include having plenty of water, food for fuel, a compass, and a map. While this list is far from exhaustive, the point to remember is that even if you are the most experienced and prepared hiker on the trail, you may find yourself in a situation that did not go as planned. Somehow, you got off your trail and no matter how hard you tried or what tools you brought, you could not get back on your own. At some point, you come to the realization that your only way out is to call for a rescue. This happened to someone I know. Thankfully, it ended with a successful outcome due to the heroic efforts of the Custer County Search and Rescue team.

He brought me up out of the pit of
destruction, out of the miry clay,
And He set my feet upon a rock making my footsteps firm.
Psalm 40:2

I teach a life skills class to folks transitioning out of incarceration. Many of these people have addictions. Most have demons. Most feel like they are living in a pit. Even though they will get released from their current confinement, they feel buried by so many barriers (financial, housing, family, addictions, etc.) that they lose hope for fear of falling back in the hole. On the last day of class, I share with them my own story. I have a lifetime of instability due to genetic issues with my joints. I share the similarities of setbacks, overcoming obstacles, hopelessness, hopefulness, and the importance of having a network of support to call on when you need help. I try to illustrate that for most, if not everyone, life does not go as planned. No matter how good the tools we each have are, most of us still wander off our path. We find ourselves stuck in a situation that we just can't get out of on our own and we need support. My story really resonated with one particular student, and we talked at length after class. He came to the conclusion that although our circumstances might be different, it doesn't really matter. Whatever your "pit" is, you feel stuck, and you just want to get out. You need to be rescued. You look for the light. I thank God that my god, my rescuer, puts my unstable feet on stable ground and establishes my path forward even when I can't walk on my own.

> *Dear Lord, please guide our hiking feet and keep us steadfastly on firm ground. Let those traversing the mountains and valleys in life find sturdy footing upon which to worship You. Guide our footsteps to Your path and keep our eyes uplifted and focused on You. In Jesus' Name, Amen.*

Date of Hike:

Climbing Party:

Notes:

CRESTONE PEAK

•••

Patience and strength. As my husband made his final push for the last two 14ers required to complete a Grand Slam, the amount of patience and strength he needed for this venture had been in the forefront of our minds. He started climbing as a twenty-something with no wife, no kids, and very little responsibility. In those first few years, summits came easy and often, and I'm sure he thought a Grand Slam would take, at most, a decade, not over three decades. As he mapped out his last routes and contemplated his big finale, the major setback of 2017 caused us to pause and reflect. What was supposed to be the completion of the remaining five peaks turned into a search and rescue, with us leaving Colorado amid unfinished business. We had to find the patience to wait another two years to attempt those last few mountains. His inability to self-rescue after he "cliffed out" shook his confidence and made him unsure in his perseverance to finish. Finding the strength in his heart to push through the instability has been a major test. He had to find a way to be calm, sure-footed, and brave enough to face another mountain with confidence.

> *You too be patient; strengthen your hearts,*
> *for the coming of the Lord is near.*
> *James 5:8*

Patience and strength are two things I need to work on in my daily life. Sometimes, I sorely lack both, and I stumble my way through the day. I like to take control. I plan out my day. I set goals. I make to-do lists. And I get impatient when things don't go as planned because other people get in my way. I get easily distracted and lose focus, often chasing the next best thing. But then I read it...this verse that talks about patience and strength. It gives me pause, and I regain my balance in a moment of silent reflection. It makes me think about paddle boarding, a favorite hobby of mine.

When I started paddle boarding, it was really hard for me. After seven knee surgeries due to hypermobility, standing on a wobbly board in the middle of a body of water was a terrifying task for me. But for whatever reason, I was up for the challenge. To say I was not graceful is an understatement. I was clumsy and crooked and could jump down to my knees very quickly to avoid a fall if a wave came my way. However, the more I practiced, the more confident I became. When I strengthened my core, I had better balance. I learned to plant my feet firmly on the board, which gave me more stability. I had to focus on a single goal and look straight ahead rather than turning my head to chat with a friend. The more I practiced, the better I became and my fears began to subside. It's taken me awhile. Balance does not come easy to me. But I persevered, strengthened my core, and as of this summer, I am able to stand up straighter and paddle through any waves that threaten to knock me down.

Dear Father, we pray for patience and strength to make it through this day. Give us hearts of perseverance to complete the tasks that You have called us to. Strengthen our hearts for whatever comes our way. Without You, we are weak; in You, we are strong. In Jesus' Name, Amen.

Date of Hike:

Climbing Party:

Notes:

CULEBRA PEAK

The only privately owned 14er in the entire United States, Culebra Peak is located in the Sangre de Cristo Mountains, Spanish for "blood of Christ." These mountains run through southern Colorado and northern New Mexico, and near San Luis, the oldest town in Colorado. This peak has had controversy over direct access and community grazing rights dating back to the days when San Luis Valley was part of Mexico. There have been three different owners of Culebra Peak since 1999 alone, but current ownership has been very accommodating to hikers, providing the party signs up online and pays the $150 access fee. A two-month summertime window, only Fridays and Saturdays available, and a limit of thirty hikers, are the unique obstacles awaiting those in their quest for Culebra. The hike itself is a ten-mile round trip trek with 4,300 feet of elevation gain. Culebra means "snake" in Spanish. This term was originally used to describe the creek near the mountain, but it perfectly describes the ridge that serpentines to the top. Distinctive for being above timberline for longer than most 14ers, its unusual identity with Spanish heritage, and its relatively easy Class 2 terrain, make it an intriguing mountain to access and climb.

In whom we have boldness and confident
access through faith in Him.
Ephesians 3:12

Prior to Jesus, only a select few—the high priests—had direct access to God. He was literally "hidden" behind the veil in the tabernacle. People actually had to make payments, in the form of offerings, to be forgiven of sins. But Jesus came to change all that. Not only did He became our personal high priest, but He also paid the price so that we might have direct access to the Father. How amazing is that! The veil has been torn in two and we are no longer restricted from meeting with the Father whenever and wherever we want.

Dear Lord, we have access to You to talk about our hopes, dreams, needs, and frustrations, and we are so thankful, but we also know we aren't telling You anything You don't already know. Yet we come to You in a posture of prayer to give our heartfelt thanks for all You do and all You have done. In Jesus' Name, Amen.

Date of Hike:

Climbing Party:

Notes:

ELLINGWOOD POINT

• •

When it comes to hiking gear, my husband has GAS, also known as Gear Acquirement Syndrome, defined as the "need" for new hiking toys. Along with GAS, he is also a Gear Head, a hiker whose main focus is backpacking and outdoor gear. This leads to being Gearly Afflicted, where no boundaries exist when it comes to acquiring new equipment. Our family motto includes: be prepared, and to my husband and sons, that means having tons of gear available at all times for all types of hikes. There is an amazing amount of hiking gear out there (and in our garage), and no limit to opinions on all of that paraphernalia. After nearly forty years of hiking, you would think my husband could just focus on the Big Three: your backpack, shelter, and sleep system. These are typically the heaviest, most pricey, and most important items carried. But with every new *Backpacker* or *Outdoor* magazine, there are new hiking items that tempt him. He scours online discussions and reviews before purchasing, but how many stuff sacks does one person really need? It makes him happy, so as long as he doesn't get too crazy, I don't intervene. I suspect it gives him some comfort because it's one of the few things he can control during his time in the backcountry. After caching items one time on Ellingwood Point that he desperately needed later in the hike, he is definitely a believer in never being separated from your gear. Family and friends have all benefited from his gear obsession over the years, and that has yielded advantageous returns and results, so no complaints have ever been voiced. Being equipped with the right gear in the backcountry is integral to a positive outcome.

All scripture is inspired by God and profitable for teaching, for reproof, for correction, for training in righteousness; so that the man of God may be adequate, equipped for every good work.
2 Timothy 3:16-17

We live in an age where we have an infinite source of knowledge literally at our fingertips. With the advent of the smartphone and the Internet, we can search for help on any given topic at any time of the day. I google *everything*. I am curious by nature, so when I have a question, I take it to Google. Sometimes, at the end of the day, I am amazed at my searches. How could my brain be so random as to question such diverse topics? What am I going to do with all of that extraneous information? Will it really make my life better knowing something or does it just become a lot of noise to distract me from what should be the guiding source of information in my life? It's true, I can't look in the Bible to see what year a certain actress was born or to recall where a line from a movie originated. But the Bible, through scripture, can and does provide the most solid guide for living the Good Life. The words in scripture teach us, through precepts and examples, how to live a righteous life. If we read and meditate upon its words, it prepares us for each and every task we will ever face.

Dear Lord, we feel exceedingly ill-equipped for the tasks which You have called us to do. But we know if You call us, You will equip us. You will equip us with the right gear, the right words, a great strength, and most importantly, grace, to carry out the goals You have laid out before us. Our capabilities and capacities will be stretched in Your service—definitely beyond our comfort zone. We thank You for enabling us to finish the assignments designated to us. In Jesus' Name, Amen.

Date of Hike:

Climbing Party:

Notes:

HUMBOLDT PEAK

● ●

I love when you are hiking and all other interferences and distractions gradually fall away. For me, the spaces where I tend to feel at peace on the hike are where the hills almost imperceptibly turn into mountains and when the timberline falls away. I love the transition places. When you are on the trail, your focus transitions from outward to inward. The physicality frees up your mind to absorb the scenery. I want to shout out to the beauty around me, but I also don't want anyone to hear me. I want to share that joy with others on the trail and those who are at home rooting for me to succeed, but I also want to keep it private. It's a struggle to want to be both unplugged and tethered to communication. You can't rely on cell phones to get in touch with fellow climbing partners at the trailhead parking lot or elsewhere on the slopes. Yet surprisingly, cell phones work splendidly on the tops of most mountains. I'm almost always able to hear my husband's loud and clear voice calling home from the tops of Colorado 14ers, California 14ers, and even state highpoints. There's nothing like hearing the excitement and joy in his voice as he shares from his summit in real time from far away.

For you will go out with joy
And be led forth with peace;
The mountains and the hills will break
forth into shouts of joy before you.
And all the trees of the field will clap their hands.
Isaiah 55:12

In my life skills class, I work with people transitioning out of the Corrections system. Many of my clients struggle with addictions, and many have recurrent lapses which end with them back in our facility, disappointed that they have failed once again. The focus of our class is to keep them from giving up hope. We teach them that even when they fall down nine times, they can get up on the tenth and try again.

I don't struggle with the same issues that they do, but that doesn't mean that I haven't had my share of falls, where I struggle to get up again. I struggle with the mountains.

You may have picked up that I (Linda) am not the best athlete. Because of degenerative knees, that was always a constant struggle. At 44, I finally got my knee replacement which I thought would completely change my disposition. And it did, to a certain degree. After working hard to rehabilitate after surgery, I set my sights on hiking with my husband and friends. I was in the best shape of my life and was excited to take on this challenge. Only, it was hard on my lungs and on my heart and, most of all, on my spirit. I found that my knees could now take me where my heart and lungs could not.

The next year, I thought if I trained harder I would succeed. But no. Once again, I felt as if I left my lungs on the side of the mountain. Year three, after doctors assured me nothing was really wrong, I tried again. This was going to be a particularly fun hike with our group. My husband, Kurt, was really looking forward to it.

I started out fine, but after a short time, I was huffing and puffing again. All I could do was focus on the back of Kurt's calves to keep me going. I was miserable, yelling and crying at myself on the inside while simultaneously trying to put on a brave face on the outside. And then—I stopped. I told Kurt and my friends to go on; I was going to turn around and not hold them back. Kurt did not want to leave me, but I insisted and won the argument (it was a well-traveled route so I would not really be alone).

I started my way down and with each step, I felt emboldened. I was moving at my own pace and my breathing slowed down. For the first time in my three years of hiking, I could look up and out. I was no longer consumed with keeping up, but instead I became more absorbed by the beauty of my surroundings.

Walking by myself at my own pace, I had no one to compare myself to so my shortcomings were not so obvious. I felt strong and empowered and I was smiling ear to ear. Passersby on the trail were obviously caught up in my joy and shouted words of encouragement as I walked by. I may have even heard a "You go girl!" It was great. One of the top days in my life! I didn't make it to the summit with everyone else that day, but I picked myself up from yet another disappointment and walked on down the mountain with no one's help but my own, and the Lord's. I love that day.

This is what I remind my students: we are *all* broken in one way or another. We *all* struggle with falling down and getting back up. I think it is when we stop trying to be on the same pace with everyone else—when we stop comparing ourselves and magnifying our shortcomings—that we begin to relax and look up and out to see the beauty around us. Not everyone will make it to the top of a 14er, but hopefully, no matter how far you go, you will feel a sense of joy, peace, and accomplishment by walking towards your own goals at your own pace.

Dear Heavenly Father, I want to praise You with my voice during times of rejoicing, as well as during times of struggle. Fill me with Your peace. Help me realize that I am performing for an audience of one, and that when I walk in Your will, it will be Your voice encouraging me along the way. In Jesus' Name, Amen.

Date of Hike:

Climbing Party:

Notes:

KIT CARSON PEAK/ CHALLENGER POINT

SOS. Help. The side of our Garmin InReach satellite phone has a flip-up cap with an easy-to-press button that directly alerts a crisis center with specific location coordinates. It should be easy, but sometimes it's hard to let go and say, "I need help." Pride, embarrassment, and stubbornness get in the way and we make the situation worse before calling out for assistance. My husband found himself in this predicament on Kit Carson Peak. We had summited Challenger Point, then I positioned myself to wait the approximately two-hour round trip for him on Kit Carson. After a successful summit, he missed the turn for Kit Carson Avenue and ended up "ledging out" on The Prow after negotiating Class 5.8 rock climbing, without rope. He could not safely down-climb from this ledge and made the call—SOS and 911. Then he hunkered down in thirty mph wind gusts on a five-by-five foot ledge waiting for the wonderful, amazing people from Custer County Search and

Rescue. As SAR was formulating a plan, another hiker made the same route-finding error and found himself on the ledge with my husband. What are the odds? While my husband was prepared to spend the night and had the clothing and provisions to do so, his new ledge-mate was not as prepared. He gently talked his new friend out of attempting the down-climb. Fortunately, SAR was able to rock climb to the stranded hikers and set up a rope belay to rappel them off The Prow. They made the right call—calling out for help. As the Incident Commander remarked, "We like these kind of outcomes."

You will seek Me and find Me
when you search for Me with all your heart.
Jeremiah 29:13

In countless situations, we all take pride in our abilities and accomplishments. We think that if we simply get stronger and gain more knowledge, we can overcome new challenges. We can have all of the tools that we think we need and the knowledge of a situation, but eventually, at some point in our lives, we *all* "ledge out." The Lord says that if we search with all of our hearts, with totality, we will find Him, even if that search for God is our last resort—an SOS—after we've exhausted all of our other possibilities and solutions. When we are able to put aside our pride and own abilities and hit the SOS button, we allow ourselves to rescued by our Savior.

Dear Lord, please help remind us to always seek You, even when there are smooth waters and smooth sailing in our lives. We tend to call out to You in times of need, but help us remember to call Your name in joyful, celebratory times as well. We are grateful for the ways we are humbled. Thank You for the gentle reminders that You are the One we give all the glory. In Jesus' Name, Amen.

Date of Hike:

Climbing Party:

Notes:

LITTLE BEAR PEAK

If ever there was a 14er that should require a helmet, it's Little Bear Peak in the Sierra Blanca Massif. The upper part of the standard route goes through the Hourglass, a 300 foot section with an almost vertical area famous for rockfall. At 14,043 feet and near the more imposing and picturesque Blanca

Peak, Little Bear is sometimes overlooked. However, most 14er climbers list Little Bear Peak as one of the most difficult. It's almost impossible to navigate through the Hourglass without dislodging some of the precambrian granite, and if there is someone following up the chute, it can be deadly. On his first attempt of Little Bear, a cousin of ours had a football-sized rock brush his side. He immediately turned back because it shook him up so much. He eventually returned and summited, choosing a weekday ascent with a super early start to avoid rocks from above. Once you hit the Hourglass, your options are very limited—you can't stay in the middle. No right turn. No left turn. Either you go up or you go down.

For the gate is small and the way is narrow that leads to life, and there are few who find it.
Matthew 7:14

We live in a world where we don't want to offend. We want to support everyone in all of their beliefs, and in the end, we take a stand for nothing. This might work for a while, until we find ourselves in a straight up ascent in life that seems impossible to climb. We need someone, something, to pull us to the other side. For me, that someone is Jesus. I know that I can only call on one god to pull me through, *the* God, Jesus Christ. He is my one and only savior. But the access to higher ground through Christ is narrow. We have to search for it. It takes effort and can be easily missed. Some folks don't want to walk through that narrow space because it might be uncomfortable and constricting. Maybe we would consider it if we could walk through with a partner, but the reality is, we can only walk through by ourselves. In fact, the passage is so narrow that we have to walk through single file. And as we walk through, we might feel a little afflicted—by family, friends, the world—all telling us there is another easier way around. But that's not truth. The only path to higher ground is through the hourglass—the path that leads to life.

Father, thank You for giving us access to higher ground through Your son, Jesus Christ. We know that following Him is the only path to life. We know that following Him might not always be easy and we have to walk alone, but we also know that this is the only access to everlasting life. In Jesus' Name, Amen.

Date of Hike:

Climbing Party:

Notes:

MOUNT LINDSEY

Summit fever is a real thing in our family. In the beginning of our hiking careers, we were focused on the top, we weren't concerned with collecting all the 14er summits. That has changed in the last decade, as my husband nears the Grand Slam milestone—standing on top of all of Colorado's 14,000 foot peaks. "Peak-bagging" seems to become more of a focus as you steadily check off the list of mountains. But back during the first dozen or so summit attempts, the focus was on having fun. One time my husband put a four pound rock in his cousin's backpack, which wasn't discovered until the summit lunch on Mount Lindsey. Needless to say, his cousin wasn't happy. Choice words followed. We often teased our sons about putting rocks in their packs to slow them down when they started acting like mountain goats, flitting up the mountain powered by youth and adrenalin. We got away from that for a while and took ourselves too seriously in the mountains, but we are back to enjoying the pure fun of hiking. There seems to be more safe shenanigans when we are in the backcountry now, like crazy summit signs, fun hidden snacks, silly buffs around our necks, and singing songs at the top of our lungs. But our favorite is still the backpack rock high up on Mount Lindsey.

Stone is heavy and the sand a burden,
but a fool's provocation is heavier than both of them.
Proverbs 27:3 (NIV)

For a while, I have walked around with a lot of baggage. It was as if I carried an imaginary backpack filled with feelings of guilt, shame and even unworthiness. We all carry around our own backpack of burdens, but this was something more. There seemed to be an extra weight that was causing me to walk with a heavier step, breathe a little harder, and grow weary more quickly. I realized I must be carrying an extra load, but I could not for the life of me identify its source. Daily in my time with God, I kept cross-examining my life, looking for what I might have said or done to offend someone to cause such guilt. I asked for forgiveness both from God and anyone I thought I might have offended. I asked God to search my heart so I could make it right. I sought the counsel of wise and trusted people.

Studying this verse gave me pause. After several years of feeling exhausted and weighed down, I realized that I had let a "fool," someone I had mistakenly trusted as a friend, slip some of her own heavy burdens out of her backpack and into mine when I wasn't paying attention. Out of her unhappiness, she spoke accusations, provoking me to react defensively and cave under the weight of her words. For a long time, I tried to shake these feelings off of my back thinking they were my own burdens I was carrying. It was not until I realized these were her burdens she imposed on me that I could finally shed the load—and some of the guilt—that I had carried for so long.

> *Dear Heavenly Father, we carry some heavy burdens. We have our own stresses and struggles we deal with on a daily basis. You promise that if we cast our burdens on You, You will help us carry them. Help me to not always feel like I have to carry others' burdens for them, but instead point them to you, the ultimate heavy lifter. In Jesus' Name, Amen.*

Date of Hike:

Climbing Party:

Notes:

ELK MOUNTAINS

CAPITOL PEAK

● ●

When hiking Colorado 14ers, one certainly uses all of the senses. The sight of majestic peaks ablaze in front of a clear blue sky; the sound of birds heralding the beginning of a hike; the feel of a well-worn performance shirt layered under fleece; the taste of a backpack flattened peanut butter and jelly sandwich at the summit; and the smell of cow pies as they crunch and squish under hiking boots. Yes, cow pies, also known as cow manure, cow pats, or cow dung, will be unexpectedly encountered on Capitol Peak. On the trail, a brush with cows and smelly manure is part of the lower elevation experience. As with many of the 14ers, a dark, early morning start is necessary for a summit bid. When the path to Capitol includes black cows on a trail dimly lit by headlamps, the senses of smell and touch are heightened. The herd, roaming in the Roaring Forks Valley, is used to hikers and therefore doesn't exit the trail when a group comes trekking. You can literally bump into a cow, and most certainly smell their presence. Capitol Peak, located in the Maroon Bells-Snowmass Wilderness of the Elk Mountain range, is one of the most dangerous 14ers in Colorado— sighting and experiencing it from the valley floor is more than enough for many mountain enthusiasts. But these bombardments of the senses all add up to make the experience that much more enjoyable...or at least memorable! The use of sight, sound, smell, touch, and taste in the mountains makes hiking a form of walking meditation. All of the distractions of daily life melt away, leaving raw and rejuvenating feelings.

*But thanks be to God, who always leads us in triumph
in Christ, and manifests through us the sweet aroma
of the knowledge of Him in every place.
2 Corinthians 2:14*

I am a person who loves perfume. My mother always gave me "Happy" for my birthday and now that she is gone, my daughters carry on her tradition by picking out a new fragrance each year that reminds them of me—of the essence that they think is me. Each morning, I take care to select the perfume that represents what I am feeling for the day. It's kind of quirky, but I give a lot of thought to what scent I give off. I never want the smell to be overbearing; rather I just want something that wafts lightly in the background. Two years ago, someone had a reaction to my perfume that etched a memory I will never forget. On the last day of my first completed session as a life skills instructor, a woman who had been somewhat negative for our twelve weeks of class came up and gave me a long, solid hug of appreciation. As she did, she visibly inhaled my aroma. "Ummm, you smell really nice. I like that." She seemed to linger a moment to take the scent in more deeply. That moment stuck with me. As I drove home, I laughed to myself, realizing the fragrance I was wearing was called "Grace." I had worked with her for weeks, trying to gain her trust and acceptance, and in the end, she smelled grace. Did she smell me or did she smell Christ seeping through my brokenness?

Dear Lord, we live in a multi-sensory world, and we humbly give thanks to You for these incredible five senses. Please help us to appreciate seeing, smelling, tasting, hearing, and touching to the fullest. Let our senses bring us closer to you. We are ever in danger of overstimulation, so please help us to stay grounded and use our senses for Your glory. In Jesus' Name, Amen.

Date of Hike:

Climbing Party:

Notes:

CASTLE PEAK

●●

When it comes down to the finish of a 14,000 foot peak, one of the best moments is calling a loved one with the incredible news that you accomplished your goal. It's the call to that person who has always believed in you and knew you had what it took, even when you doubted yourself. For my husband, this person was his dad, Scotty. Although they were fortunate enough to hike a 14er together once, all of the other sixty-plus peaks my husband has done in Colorado and California were with other people. No matter what, Grandpa Scotty was the first person he called. Since he himself summited a 14,000 foot peak, he was keenly aware of the time and exertion needed to get to the top. It really honed an appreciation for what my husband was accomplishing. The first peak my husband climbed after his father passed away was one of the saddest. He wanted to share his good news with one of his biggest fans, and give an update on his quest for a Colorado Grand Slam. Many of our climbing partners have accomplished a 14er Grand Slam in a few short years. My husband is needing over thirty years to finish his goal, which is pretty remarkable since he has never lived in Colorado and must make the trek there to acclimate and climb. On climbs, he still longs to call and spread the good news with his loved one that is no longer with us.

How lovely on the mountains
Are the feet of him who brings good news,
Who announces peace
And brings good news of happiness,
Who announces salvation,
And says to Zion,"Your God reigns!"
Isaiah 52:7

I hate the thought of evangelizing. It gives me sweaty palms just thinking about it. My grandmother used to hand out religious tracts wherever she went. This caused me angst and embarrassment as a child. I think of evangelizing as a formal process, sitting down to systematically explain the Gospel to a non-believer, trying to convince someone that my way of believing is the right way and theirs is wrong. I run away from that!

But I do love to share my joy with people. I love to share the good things that are happening as a result of God's work in my life—not as a way of bragging, but as an overflow of the heart. My husband, friends, and co-workers have walked with me through some pretty lonely places of my life. They know those hard parts of my story, and I am so glad. But I don't want to be known only for that—I want people to see the joy I experience both *in* and *despite* my hardships. I want to shout the joy from the mountaintops that I experience as a testimony that the sorrow I have felt is far from the end of the story. Although it looks far different from the tracts that my grandma used to share, I guess I too am eager to share the Good News.

Father, help me to have a heart for sharing the Good News. Help me not to be afraid or embarrassed of the good work You have done in my life, but instead, help me shout it from the mountaintops and always give glory to You! In Jesus' Name, Amen.

Date of Hike:

Climbing Party:

Notes:

MAROON PEAK

The heart skips a beat. As soon as I emerged from the car for a hike to rendezvous with my husband's 14er climbing group, I saw them. Two helicopters circling the valley along the trail to the Maroon Bells. I knew that the party had summited thanks to a phone call, but no cell service in the park meant no communication since. The two choppers, Black Hawks, were making figure 8's around the steep slopes way up on the

118

mountains. After a few passes, they would fly down and up the valley and then hover and circle some more. The sound and the pattern were reminiscent of angry hornets disturbed from their nests. Over and over, they circled. I feared for the climbing party I was meeting at Crater Lake while rain and sleet pelted down. The nerves set in again knowing that the slick, rotten rock of the Bells needs no added moisture to be treacherous. And it was cold...very cold for early August. The group was properly equipped, but worry set in. Then, one of those "God moments" happened. The clouds parted, the sun shined brief but strong, and I knew everything was going to be okay. The fact that the helicopters were working so diligently meant there was a *rescue* to be made—not a *recovery*. That's a huge distinction. Whatever had happened, there was hope. Our party arrived safely intact at the rendezvous point and we prayed for the people who were in need of rescuing. It was an intense day of climbing for my husband and his climbing buddies. A near lightning strike, route-finding challenges, wind, and snow added to the stress of the twelve-hour day on the mountain.

Return, O LORD, rescue my soul;
Save me because of Your lovingkindness.
Psalm 6:4

Some days are hard. Some seasons of my life, I am lost. Challenging circumstances cloud my perception and put me in positions that literally suck the life out of me. Subtle changes in my life can knock me off the path before I even know it. A dark cloud can last a few hours, sometimes a few days, or even weeks. And feeling lost can cause a separation from my family and friends—and even God. Family and friends may notice my "funk," but can't really say or do anything to get me out of it. That's when I need a search and rescue. When I call out to the Lord, He is able to refresh my soul, to remove the cloud, help me catch my breath, and feel alive again. It is because of His goodness that He continues to do figure 8's around my life. It is because of His kindness that He hovers until I look up and see what was bogging me down. And it is because of His faithfulness that He never gives up pursuing me until He delivers me safely back on the path.

> *Dear Lord, You have rescued us from so many known and unknown dangers, and we are eternally grateful. Our hearts continually search for You whether in the wilderness or civilization. We are blessed beyond any understanding for the lovingkindness You give us. Thank you for being our Savior. In Jesus' Name, Amen.*

Date of Hike:

Climbing Party:

Notes:

NORTH MAROON PEAK

· ·

Words are so powerful, but when we picture hiking and being amongst nature in the mountains, we usually think of quiet and serene solitude—a literal hush of all speech. However, communication is arguably more important in backcountry settings. Having complete and total confidence in your hiking partner's verbal and non-verbal communication skills is imperative for a successful hike. Especially when climbing with ropes, predetermined phrases and hand signals are essential for safety. It all comes down to exchanging information in a timely manner, and is so important when belaying or rappelling with a partner. On steep sections, like the chimney on North Maroon Peak, ropes can offer extra protection for hikers. North Maroon, a 14,014 foot peak in the Elk Range, is complicated and exposed. Using a rope on its short, steep hourglass section can reduce a little danger. There are specific phrases that must be said to keep all parties safe during the process. Some examples of the basics are:

Climber: *"On Belay?"* Am I on belay, I want to start climbing, do you have me?

Belayer: *"Belay on!"* The belayer is anchored in and has the rope set up through her belay device. She calls this command to let the climber know she's ready to belay.

Climber: *"Climbing!"* The climber signals that she is ready to start climbing.

Belayer: *"Climb on!"* The belayer again signals she is ready for the climber.

Climber: *"Slack!"* The climber needs extra rope in order to make the first move or to finish taking apart her belay anchor.

Climber: *"Up rope!"* The climber no longer needs the slack in the rope. Asks belayer to take it in. This can be used at any point in the climb to signal to the belayer to take up the slack.

These are commands that cannot be confused. They are not tentative questions, but charges with clear, specific meanings. Communication is key.

> *And behold, you shall be silent and unable to speak*
> *until the day when these things take place,*
> *because you did not believe my words,*
> *which will be fulfilled at the proper time.*
> *Luke 1:20*

Zechariah was an old priest when the angel came to tell him his wife would be expecting a child. As a priest, he would have been a learned man in the scriptures and prophecies of the Old Testament. If anyone should have trusted the words of the angel, it should have been Zechariah. After all, he spent his whole life looking for clues that would point to the Messiah. Yet, when told what was coming, he didn't believe. He questioned the angel. And he was punished. His words were taken from him until the time of John's birth. Have you ever wondered why? Perhaps Zechariah spent his whole life "talking the talk"—teaching about the scriptures and prophecies to those who would listen. By rendering him mute, Zechariah now had to "walk the walk." Now his actions would have to demonstrate his belief in God and prayer rather than just his words. How are you demonstrating your faith? Are you just "talking the talk" about your belief in God and prayer, or are you also "walking the walk?"

> *Dear Father, I pray that I lead by example in*
> *my walk of faith. Help me understand that I need*
> *to walk the walk and not just talk the talk. I want*
> *to be a more authentic example of what it means*
> *to be a follower of Christ. In Jesus' Name, Amen.*

Date of Hike:

Climbing Party:

Notes:

PYRAMID PEAK

The climbing party of three got slightly off route near the triangular summit of Pyramid Peak. To say the route finding was extremely difficult would be an understatement. There are no distinguishing characteristics to any of the reddish-brown rock that gives the appearance of scorched earth. Extreme exposure and loose rocks, crumbly and "rotten," also make this standard route one of the most difficult and dangerous of all the 14ers. The group carefully and systematically made their way up the Class 4 terrain. Protection using ropes would be ideal, but the flaky rock makes that impossible. Instead, my husband and his partners would reach up above them and feel for a rock—any rock—that might be stable enough to grab and pull their weight up a few more feet. The climb is arduous, tedious, and most definitely scary. The search for adequate handholds unnerves my husband, who remembers trying five, six, seven, or more rocks before he felt confident enough to creep higher. The climb up leaves him shaken, as shaky as those rocks he just scaled. Looking at the summit shots from that day, this point is driven home. There is grave concern on my husband's face and on the face of his long-time hiking buddy. The down-climb was going to be worse. The third climber in their group did not fully grasp the gravity of the situation, his face is blissfully ecstatic in the photos. Thankfully, they were able to find the best route for the descent. It was far less harrowing than they anticipated. They were able to scramble down without incident.

And the LORD will continually guide you,
And satisfy your desire in scorched places,
And give strength to your bones;
And you will be like a watered garden,
And like a spring of water whose waters do not fail.
Isaiah 58:11

Some seasons in my life have left me scorched and spiritually dry. It would be easy to say this happened only when times got tough. However, the truth is, I usually become spiritually dry when I am running a race with no end, operating daily at such a frenetic pace that I don't take time to pause and look up. During a week when I was running at a particularly fast pace, not taking time for any self-care or feeding of my soul, I literally stumbled into this verse.

The verse says that the LORD will *continually* guide me. The Hebrew word for "continually" is "tamiyd," meaning perpetuity, always, constantly...to stretch. I never would have guessed the meaning of that word. It says that the LORD will continually *stretch* to lead me...in *perpetuity.* For me, that is a reminder that the LORD is reaching out for me...stretching to reach *for me.* All I have to do is grab on in order to receive His guidance. He is not asking me to lead. He is not asking me to pursue Him. He is just asking me to grab on. Reading that relieves the burden of having to do one more thing in my day. Knowing that I just have to *receive* refreshes my soul and gives me renewed strength.

Dear Lord, thank You for Your continued guidance, wherever we may roam. Be it the highest peaks or the lowest valleys, the protection You provide is more than we could ever ask. Thank You for the strength to complete the tasks You have placed in our path and for the companions You have called to gently guide us when we have gotten off route. We are eternally grateful for this. In Jesus' Name, Amen.

Date of Hike:

Climbing Party:

Notes:

SNOWMASS MOUNTAIN

Snowmass Mountain is a shy mountain. It's nearly impossible to see from any road. Nine miles of trekking over horse-trodden, messy, hard-to-find trail, and it still remains elusive. It wants to remain out of sight and out of reach. Yet, it taunts you with promises of beautiful views and amazing vistas. It was almost painful to realize it was evasive and out of reach, but we actually took the most spectacular photos of the sunrise and wildflowers without coming anywhere near the mountain. It was truly some of the most jaw-dropping terrain we have ever seen, and we have photographs to prove it. On our first attempt, the summit remained out of reach due to weather, but the elusiveness only added to its charm. Two years later, the climbers got to see Snowmass Mountain's amazing view from the top.

...that they would seek God,
if perhaps they might grope for Him and find Him,
though He is not far from each one of us...
Acts 17:27

How often do we search for God and He seems elusive? We pray to Him, only we don't hear His response. We look for signs of Him, like a burning bush, only to come up empty. Sometimes, it's as if we are children, groping our way down a hallway in the darkest part of the night, trying to feel our way for any recognizable signs that will reaffirm that we are heading in the right direction. Sometimes we are too busy praying—or rather doing the talking *to* God—or waiting for a prophetic sign. We don't understand that He is really right here with us—all the time, even in the small stuff. In our search, we need to recognize His features, His character, His voice—and then we will begin to recognize Him all around us. Indeed, when we quietly seek Him, we will find him, for He is with us.

Father, we praise You for being a God who is always with Your people. We pray that You give us eyes to see and ears to hear Your distinguishing presence in our everyday life. In our search to know You, let us quiet our voices and still our hearts to recognize You are near. In Jesus' Name, Amen.

Date of Hike:

Climbing Party:

Notes:

SAN JUAN MOUNTAINS

EL DIENTE PEAK

It was a glorious day when my husband completed his 14er Grand Slam by summiting El Diente Peak in southwest Colorado. His faithful climbing buddy/cousin repeated El Diente so my better half didn't have to solo the peak. Since my husband had "ledged out" on another mountain while climbing alone, it was my wish—new family rule—that he find someone to scramble up the Class 3 rocky trail. It had been fifteen years since his cousin had finished his own Grand Slam (coincidently, finishing on the same peak) and he was a little reluctant to return. But his sense of loyalty and devotion to family led him to accompany my husband up one of the hardest 14ers. It was a rough twelve-hour day. Several times during the hike, both parties were unsure if success was possible. My husband forgot his boot insoles. His cousin had just started wearing glasses, and found that his depth perception was skewed (on steep sections depth perception is hugely important). But they refused to separate and endured to make it to the top. The summit photos are awesome, but the pictures snapped when they returned to the vehicle show the relief and camaraderie they felt in making an incident-free round trip together. In 2010, a fatality occurred on El Diente and the victim's dog stood guard overnight until Search and Rescue could perform a recovery. These types of stories are numerous in the climbing community. Faithful hiking friends and dogs, out of true love and pure devotion, make sacrifices of time and energy to spur their loved ones to the top or comfort them in times of need. Having someone jump in the valley trenches and climb lofty peaks with you can be the difference between success and failure. It's the ultimate sign of authentic allegiance and love.

"Greater love has no one than this,
that one lay down his life for his friends."
John 15:13

This verse just makes me love Jesus. In a chapter that is riddled with metaphor, He makes this point plain and simple: there is no greater love than to lay down one's life for one's friends. In context, He is asking this of His disciples. In actuality, He is doing this Himself. Each time I examine the wording, more is revealed as to just what Jesus gave up for me. The Greek word for life is "psuche," meaning breath, breath of life, the soul, and eternal blessedness. I have never taken the time to fully ponder that deeply. He gave up His life, yes, but He also gave up His eternal blessedness. He allowed Himself to be separated from God the Father—for me. He gave up His soul, His desires. Would I do the same for Him? Do I do the same for Him? *No.* I am embarrassed to admit that some days I won't even lay aside my desire for what we watch on Netflix that night. That's me, selfish. And Him, selfless.

Dear Jesus, help me to never forget the sacrificial love You have for me. Help me to have a heart like Yours. Help me to look for those opportunities where I can lay down my life, not only for You, but also my friends. Let Your sacrificial love be a constant reminder of how to live my life each day. In Jesus' Name, Amen.

Date of Hike:

Climbing Party:

Notes:

MOUNT EOLOUS

•••

Mount Eolous, part of the Needle Mountains of the Rockies, is located near Durango in southwest Colorado. Eolous is named after the Greek god of wind, Aelolus, and was originally spelled that way until 1878. Random checks of weather conditions on the peak revealed sustained winds at twenty to thirty mph, high enough to unnerve you when standing on an exposed ridge. Eolous, along with its neighbors Sunlight Peak and Windom Peak, are some of the most remote 14ers. It's rated as a Class 3 hike, which means it includes rock scrambling. Hikes are classified by a system known as Yosemite Decimal System, using numbers and decimals 1 through 5—Class 1 being the least steep and exposed, all the way to Class 5, being vertical in steepness, completely unprotected from severe weather, and featuring sheer drop-offs. Though Mount Eolous is a Class 3, there is a catwalk near the end after a steep hike that will take your breath away, even on a windless day.

*"The wind blows where it wishes, and you hear the sound of it,
but do not know where it comes from and where it is
going; so is everyone who is born of the Spirit."*
John 3:8

My husband had the amazing experience of helping a friend on his quest for a 14er Grand Slam. Our friend had been diagnosed at a young age with MS and wanted to complete as many peaks in Colorado as he could. He also wanted to rock climb as many prominent features of the Sandia Mountains of New Mexico as possible. Knowing his climbing days were very limited sparked our friend into action and drove him to complete bucket list items. One mission included my husband leading an expedition group consisting of our friend, his father, and his three friends. It was a special time helping a climbing buddy reach his goals. After completing a Colorado Grand Slam, he focused on Sandia's big rock climbing walls. He wanted his children in Albuquerque to lift their eyes to the east and know their father had conquered the roughest and toughest of them. It was an honor to be on those wind-swept walls with him when he reached his goal.

Dear Lord, as we make our plans and set our courses, we ask You to direct each step, lest we be distracted by where the wind blows. Lead us to the goals You have set forth for us and help us to use Your word as a blueprint. With each step, help us seek Your guidance. In Jesus' Name, Amen.

Date of Hike:

Climbing Party:

Notes:

HANDIES PEAK

Handies Peak was our first 14,000 foot summit attempt after my husband's need of Custer County Search and Rescue from a ledge on Kit Carson Peak. To say I was suffering from post-traumatic stress is an understatement. The experience of watching a hero of mine in need of help was humbling for both of us, plus the extreme duress of hiking alone for six hours still lingers with me. We really got in touch with our humanness that day. Yet, we felt the best way to put the August 2017 incident behind us was to literally get back on the saddle—the saddle ridge to Handies Peak. The mountain is considered one of the more straight-forward ascents, and we picked it for that reason. We could have put 14er climbing behind us, or at least taken a break for a while, but we didn't want to get stuck in a roundabout of comfort, familiarity, and relative safety. There was pushback from family and a few friends. But as God guided our footsteps to success, we felt the risk was worth taking as we stood atop that summit and rejoiced.

May the God of hope fill you with all joy
and peace as you trust in him,
so that you may overflow with hope by
the power of the Holy Spirit.
Romans 15:13 (NIV)

We live in a world that is so broken. I am reminded of this every day when I teach in our county Department of Corrections. I work with people who struggle with addictions and have been convicted of felonies. Almost all of my students come from a cycle of poverty, abuse, and/or addictions that have been handed down to them from their families. I teach a class on life skills in the workplace, but really it is a class on instilling hope. My teaching team and I try to get students to see the unique strengths that they have developed from surviving very adverse situations. We want them to see that they can use those strengths to propel forward and create a more positive future for themselves.

My class is secular so I don't talk openly about my faith as part of the curriculum. But my students know that it is because of my faith that I volunteer to teach. To build a level of trust with them, I become very transparent about my day-to-day struggles and insecurities, but I do so with a level of peace and joy that seems to fill them with hope. Since my god is the God of hope and I put my trust in Him each day, each week on my drive to class, I pray for the strength of the Holy Spirit to guide me in my words and discussions. And to my amazement, I am filled with a peace that overflows to my students. Usually one of them will share their story of peace and we will *all* be filled to overflowing. Before you know it, hope begins to penetrate the room. Where do you put your hope?

> *Dear Lord, we ask You to be with all members of Search and Rescue teams and all first responders. They are there for people in times of need, and we are so grateful for them. They put their lives on the line daily for complete strangers and we are so thankful for their selflessness. Remind us to follow their example in our daily lives and reflect the hope and trust we have in You. In Jesus' Name, Amen.*

Date of Hike:

Climbing Party:

Notes:

REDCLOUD PEAK

Lightning is one of the most dangerous aspects of high-altitude hiking. The problem with bad weather in the mountains is that you can be in the shadow of a large peak, and it's very difficult, if not impossible, to see what is over the next ridge. Storms can pop up quickly and with sketchy cell service deep in the backcountry, weather apps might not be useable. If you hike in Colorado in the summer, it's almost guaranteed that afternoon storms will develop and precautions need to be taken. One rule of thumb is to set a drop-dead turnaround time. Summiting by noon is a great idea. Depending on the time of year and the weather patterns, if you haven't reached the top by 12 o'clock, stop wherever you are on the mountain and descend. This can be a difficult decision when you are 1000, 500, or even 200 feet from the top, but it is truly better to be safe than sorry. Lightning and storms can be deadly, and the peak will always be there for climbing another day. If you find yourself in a thunderstorm, the only course of action is to get down off the mountain as quickly as possible. Unfortunately, in over thirty years of hiking, we have witnessed strikes on Redcloud, hair standing on end on Mount Massive, and had our faces tingling on the Bells—definitely something to avoid. Make sure your hiking plans allow for weather changes.

Be on the alert, stand firm in the faith,
act like men, be strong.
Let all that you do be done in love.
1 Corinthians 16:13-14

Many of us go through seasons in our lives where we find ourselves on a smooth path with no real obstacles to hinder our journey. But sometimes, too much of a good thing can also lead to self-destruction if we are not careful. When the path is smooth, we may pick up the pace and walk with abandon. We may be pursuing one goal when suddenly many other great and worthy opportunities also come along. We may think these invitations will propel us towards our long term goal, but in reality, too many of these worthy invitations can lead to a frenzied schedule, leaving us little margin when unforeseen circumstances arise. I'm writing this in January—a time of re-set for many. The recurring theme I hear among young moms is the need to simplify—to say no, even to the good things. Too many positive opportunities and enjoyable activities have left these moms feeling frazzled. Literally I have heard the phrase "my hair on fire." To be sure, it can be hard to say no—to turnaround. We have to decide which activities or invitations we can say no to so we don't get derailed from our primary goal and still leave us with our hair intact. This is when we must stand firm in our faith that God will guide us towards the *best* things. We must ask the Father for guidance; stand firm in our convictions which will ultimately make us stronger; and deliver our "no's" in love for those who have extended the invitation.

Dear Lord, in all things, we give You thanks. We especially thank You for the adrenaline that helps us stand alert to present dangers. It serves us well in the mountains. Thank You for the discernment to consider finishing a hike or returning another day. We are able to stand firm in our faith and be strong since You have equipped us so well. Thank You for loving us so we can, in turn, do all things with love for our family, friends, and fellow hikers. In Jesus' Name, Amen.

Date of Hike:

Climbing Party:

Notes:

SAN LUIS PEAK

• •

It takes tremendous courage to set foot on a 14er trail, and that is certainly amplified when it necessitates a pre-dawn start. Walking through dense forest surrounded by darkness and mysterious sounds takes mental and physical strength. With only a small spotlight from a headlamp illuminating the path, we started our long hike on San Luis forging ahead on faith. It is eerie, but also oddly calming. The trail is usually fairly well-marked near the trailhead so you easily follow the path, freeing your mind to ponder the many steps ahead. Sometimes, you are truly almost alone on the mountain, as was the case on San Luis Peak. Only seven people summited on our hike day and it remains one of my favorite peaks because of that isolation. The solitude is perfect for reflection, prayer, and to be in quiet awe of the beauty God made in the formation of mountains. Being able to replicate Jesus' solitude in prayer was truly amazing.

> *In the early morning, while it was still dark,*
> *Jesus got up, left the house, and went away to a*
> *secluded place, and was praying there.*
> *Mark 1:35*

Scripture tells us that Jesus got up very early in the morning, in the fourth watch, sometime between 3 and 6 a.m, and definitely before the sun was up. During that time, He may have been the only one awake, going to a secluded place to pray. Isn't that strange? Most of the people that I have ever talked to who have trouble sleeping report this restlessness of their souls occurs around 3 a.m. Minds fill with anxiety of endless to-do lists that will never be fully accomplished or of worries about health, finances, and children. At least that is my experience. I find myself alone with my thoughts, just laying in bed allowing them to fester. Why don't I just get up—just do it as swiftly as He does, and pray? Why don't I talk to God as Jesus did during that fourth watch of the night? Why don't I go to that secluded place that calls to me? The Greek word for secluded is eremos. The definitions range from solitary and desolate to an uncultivated region fit for pasture or *feeding*. Is God calling me during that fourth watch to feed my soul? What a beautiful thought.

Father, when my soul is restless during the darkest hours of the night, nudge me to get up, leave the bed, and head to a place of prayer where my spirit will be fed. In Jesus' Name, Amen.

Date of Hike:

Climbing Party:

Notes:

MOUNT SNEFFELS

Technically, it is possible to complete a 14er Grand Slam without using climbing rope. However, many people prefer the extra assurance provided by anchors, nylon webbing, metal bolts and other types of protection. Several peaks, including Mount Sneffels, have sections where roping up makes sense to those of us who are not as comfortable with steepness and exposure. Taking a rock climbing class is recommended, and practicing to get comfortable with your gear is a must. We practiced on Cow Call Wall in the Jemez Mountains of New Mexico. It's a perfect set-up to apply your knowledge. You can walk around behind the wall on a gentle slope to secure your webbing and ropes to practice belaying and rappelling. After months of rehearsal, rock climbing up on Mount Sneffels became a reality. There is much to learn about climbing roped-up, but one point stands out. Anchors are strongest when *three points* of contact are attached and secured to the rock surface. There are numerous types of rock surfaces on Colorado 14ers, ranging from very stable to "rotten" or crumbly and very unstable, making it difficult to anchor yourself safely to the mountain. Study the terrain and master the technique before attempting climbing with rope.

This hope we have as an anchor to the soul,
a hope both sure and steadfast.
Hebrews 6:19

All of us are going to experience similar circumstances throughout our life. We will all be born. We will experience sickness, whether directly or indirectly. We will witness beauty. We will have triumphs, as well as set-backs. And we will experience death. That is true whether Christian or non-Christian. In a world full of contradictions and daily bad news reflecting the instability of the world, how are we not to just fall into a pit if we are standing on shaky ground? As Christians, we have two things that we can rest upon to anchor our souls on a firm foundation. We are assured of God's unchanging nature and His promises to us. "Because God wanted to make the unchanging nature of his purpose very clear to the heirs of what was promised, he confirmed it with an oath." Hebrews 6:17 (NIV). These truths allow us to be anchored in a hope that no matter how shaky the ground may be beneath our feet, we are anchored to Him. How can we anchor ourselves to Him so that we can feel secure in our times of need? Study His word. Reflect on His nature. Meditate on His promises. Putting these disciplines into practice allows us to feel secure in His hope for us.

Dear Lord, we thank You for Your protection when we are standing on shaky ground, and we rejoice in the anchoring You provide us, both sure and steadfast. As we study Your word more and more, we appreciate and treasure the promises You have made. Please hear our heartfelt cries as we feel secure in our faith in You. In Jesus' Name, Amen.

Date of Hike:

Climbing Party:

Notes:

SUNLIGHT PEAK

Sometimes I'm not so inclined to prepare for the incline. I know I need to get some mileage under my feet, but the motivation is lacking. Then I remember the amazing scenery experienced on past hikes, or recall the sound of pine needles crunching under my hiking boots, or the reflection of a peak on a glassy mountain lake high up on the hillside, and I get moving. There are many beautiful spots near the 14ers with lakes in the foreground and towering peaks in the background. Chicago Basin, in the southwest corner of Colorado, has magnificent views of three 14,000 foot peaks from twin lakes located at 12,500 feet. Sunlight Peak, Windom Peak, and Mount Eolus are often climbed together and are some of the most remote mountains in the state. No roads lead to the trailhead so it is usually accessed by train, but the journey is well worth it. The lake reflection of these spectacular peaks and their flower-covered grassy slopes is awe-inspiring.

As in water face reflects face,
So the heart of man reflects man.
Proverbs 27:19

When I look at my reflection in the mirror each morning, what do I see? Often, I am looking hard at the imperfections, even magnifying them so I can focus on them. I don't see myself as God sees me, as one of his image bearers—a reflection of Himself.

When I look at my heart, what do I see? What are the inner thoughts running through my mind that no one else can hear? What are the appetites that I incline my heart to? Is it my work? My husband? My kids? Even my grandkids? Although those can be good and noble things, they can quickly become idols if I give them my prime time and devotion. If I don't incline myself to the Lord first and foremost, I won't get to experience the richness of walking with Him. I want to be in relationship with Him *first* because I want my life and my heart to reflect all of His goodness, making the scenery of my life—my work, my husband, my kids, my grandkids—all the more spectacular.

> *Father, help me to have a heart that reflects You. When people look at my life, I pray that they see You. Let my thoughts, words, and deeds be a daily reflection of the role that You play in my life. In Jesus' Name, Amen.*

Date of Hike:

Climbing Party:

Notes:

SUNSHINE PEAK

•••

The very best part about finishing a 14er, or any hike for that matter, is the first taste of "real food" after a long day of exertion— not an apple, or granola, or a protein bar, but something to splurge on after your journey is over. For those of us who are always thinking about our next meal, a long, arduous hike gives us plenty of time to consider what restaurant to hit after the big hike. Guaranteed, it will be the best hamburger/pizza/taco/etc. that you have ever consumed. We found ourselves at Cannibal Grill in Lake City after hiking Sunshine Peak and the burger was awesome. Beau Jo's Pizza in Idaho Springs is another post-hike favorite in the mountaineering community. The amount of calories burned on any given trek varies, but one thing is for sure: your appetite will be at an all-time high. Another incentive strategy is the summit snack. It's a hugely important choice and must be planned accordingly. My personal favorite: Pringles. The packaging is perfect for stuffing in a backpack and the salt-to-grease ratio rocks. When the focus is on food, the extreme exertion lessens...a little.

Go then, eat your bread in happiness
and drink your wine with a cheerful heart;
for God has already approved your works.
Ecclesiastes 9:7

Growing up, I was taught to always work hard and be humble. We didn't have a lot of money, and my father didn't care at all for braggarts. Although we had some laughter in my family, we had many more somber times that called for me to be serious. From my late teens through my forties, it seemed as though I was *always* planning funerals (one per decade, in fact). I became really pretty good at gathering people together to mourn, hosting a celebration of life while staying within our limited means.

So when it came to planning my daughters' weddings, I was out of my element. I felt so guilty for planning *joyous* celebrations. Instead of enjoying the moment, I kept living in "what if" moments. I thought more about who wouldn't be around the table instead of who would be there to celebrate with us. It's hard to admit, but I often cried out of guilt for feeling happy. Consequently, I often imagined problems that didn't exist and conflicts that never arose. We were planning beautiful weddings for my girls, but by the national averages, they were not extravagant. Still, I felt the incessant need to justify each decision we made and every detail we chose, nearly sucking the joy out of my girls' engagements.

One afternoon when I was particularly weepy, I drove to a nearby lake for some quiet time. I was leafing through my Bible and stumbled upon Ecclesiastes. I needed that book right then. The words leapt off the page as if God Himself was instructing me to go and enjoy this sweet time of celebration. He was telling me that He *delights* in our joy. It is part of His plan for us. He wants us to enjoy our lives as well.

Dear Lord, we pray for wisdom each day. We pray for the wisdom and energy to work for Your glory, and we thank You for the wonderful sustenance You provide for us to energize and mobilize. We pray for the wisdom to fully enjoy and partake in all that You have given us—food, shelter, water, and working hands. We truly thank You for all of the simple joys in life, whether it is walking to our car or walking up a peak over 14,000 feet high. In Jesus' Name, Amen.

Date of Hike:

Climbing Party:

Notes:

UNCOMPAHGRE PEAK

●●●

Sweat now, summit later. In the bleak month of January; that mantra has to be front and center in my mind. We are fortunate enough to live in a community with miles and miles of great hiking trails. In that same community, ten inches of snowfall can stay on the ground for three weeks at a time. Day after day we tried to get some 14er training miles in. On the first day, the ice forced us to turn around after mile one. The next day the deep water that wasn't draining stopped us at mile two. On the third day, a tree had fallen at the three-mile turnaround point, blocking our path and any chance of a big mileage day. The temperature hovered in the upper 20s on all of those days. The January goal of 100 miles remained unmet—logging a dismal sixty-four miles by the end of the month. Essentially, we were sixty-four percent successful which is a letter grade "D." Training for a bold ascent like Uncompahgre Peak is going to take an "A" grade. Uncompahgre is Colorado's sixth highest peak. For many people it might not be considered bold, but for some it is. While roping up isn't necessary, the trail gets interesting as it dodges cliffs around the 14,000 foot mark, and trail finding is essential. At various turns, the trail is hidden and it's hard to be sure that you're on the right path. Determination and the right mindset are needed to accomplish this summit.

Now faith is the assurance of things hoped for,
the conviction of things not seen.
Hebrews 11:1

My faith has really been a journey into the unknown for me throughout my entire life. I remember heading into surgery as a young girl. As I was waiting alone in that in-between space of leaving my parents behind at the doors while waiting to get into the operating room, I remember the profound sense of God being with me, holding my hand. I didn't have an epiphany at that moment, just a calming sense of His presence.

Looking back, I don't think I've ever had a moment where I officially accepted Christ into my heart. There is not a specific day I can pinpoint to on my calendar, despite the fact that I grew up in Church, went through Confirmation, and am still actively going to Church. But there are moments in my life where I can say without a doubt, "Yes, He was there." Over the course of my life, the moments became more frequent and eventually I was confident that He and I were walking together daily.

My husband likes to use the analogy of a lake freezing in winter. The lake starts out liquid, but over time it solidifies until you can walk on it without fear of falling in. Just when that solidifying moment happens is a mystery to us nonscientific folk, but when it happens, you are assured that what is underfoot is solid. That is exactly how I describe my faith. I don't know exactly when it happened, but after years of walking with Him, I too am assured that I'm walking on solid ground.

Dear Father, give us hearts of faith. Let us keep pursuing You, even when we don't fully understand. Help us follow You even when the path seems unsure to us, resting in the confidence that when we follow You, we walk on solid ground. In Jesus' Name, Amen.

Date of Hike:

Climbing Party:

Notes:

WETTERHORN PEAK

● ●

Ten magnificent days in colorful Colorado is the perfect way to set yourself up for 14er success, leaving plenty of time for acclimating, finding trailheads, and enjoying the sights. One year on our annual trek to the Rockies, we accidentally experienced the aspens in their full fall glory. We had never seen those incredible trees at their peak color. For nine days, including summit day, we had picture-perfect "bluebird" weather, no clouds during most of the daylight hours and just a few late evening showers. However, following our summit day, the clouds rolled in during the night and a steady rain fell from the sky into the next day. As we were navigating Engineer's Pass, a four-wheel drive road west of Lake City, we saw many more stands of aspens. To our astonishment, they looked even more vibrant, colorful, and spectacular than they did on the clearer days. It was bewilderingly beautiful as the leaves had more tinting and brightness in diffused, cloudy lighting than in full sunlight. It was mesmerizing. Our many photographs reveal what we witnessed. Although they could never capture the true splendor, our cloudy aspen photos are more stunning than the sun-drenched pictures taken just days before. We still marvel at the fact that ninety percent of our Colorado vacation featured blue skies, but our most vivid memories are of that one overcast day.

Let your light shine before men
in such a way that they may see your good works,
and glorify your Father who is in heaven.
Matthew 5:16

Why is it that our eyes immediately turn to those objects that are shiny or bright? I could be walking through a forest covered in decaying leaves and still manage to see a dime shining through the darkness. Like a moth, I am drawn and captivated by the light.

Driving through Colorado last fall, I was mesmerized by the beauty of the trees. As the miles passed, I noticed the brilliance of the groves of aspens that were magnificent in their sheer number. But I was equally drawn to the individual aspens that stood out in their brilliance amongst a grove of pines.

It's probably strange, but I find a lot of similarities between myself and the aspens. I love that the bark of this tree can become rough, dry, and cracked with age. I admire the resilience they have to the forces of nature they endure. That is why you see so many groves in the Central Rockies; they can often survive where other trees are destroyed. I long to hear the aspens quake. Folklore suggests that if you lay beneath a grove of trees, you can hear the leaves almost whisper as they shake.

I want to be like the lone aspen, shining in the midst of some not so shiny things. I want to be resilient. It seems like the world is becoming void of hope and joy. The news is so depressing, and fear and anxiety seem to be wiping people out. I want to be the shiny object, albeit a little rough and cracked with age, but also resilient to what life throws my way. I want to stand out and point to the glorious works that the Father has done in my life. I want to point to hope. I want to point to Him.

Father, help me to shine my light wherever I am so that people may see Your goodness. I am broken and fissured from the world, but I hope that when people look at me, they see the goodness and light shining through that is only from You. May my light be a witness to the transformative work You have done in my life. In Jesus' Name, Amen.

Date of Hike:

Climbing Party:

Notes:

MOUNT WILSON

On one of my first climbs, I found myself clinging to a boulder on a steep ledge while wind swirled around me. I was unsteady and frozen in place. A question kept repeating in my mind, "Do I have what it takes to make it down on my own?" The up climb was a little dicey, but the down climb was making my hair stand on end. My husband had a similar experience on Mount Wilson where the exposed final summit ridge is the last barrier to the top. A lot of people rope-up for that section. These are the moments that really test you. Even the most experienced and safety-conscience climbers have been caught in unfortunate circumstances with steep exposure on trails, rock walls, and ice falls. Several yearly publications recount accidents and give tips to avoid similar experiences. It's part of the adventure—knowing there are risks can be one of the reasons why some people are drawn to the sport in the first place. There are those of us who crave the adrenaline rush of living on the virtual edge and clinging to a mountain. And there are those of us who do not. I definitely fall into the second camp. I will never forget clinging to that windswept rock, literally giving it the biggest bear hug. I felt like the wind was going to dislodge me at any moment. But I dug deep and made it down. I've never had a similar experience on a 14er, but I've had other times when my hair stood on end, and I clung to the mountains knowing that I could get knocked off my balance at any moment.

My soul clings to You; Your right hand upholds me.
Psalms 63:8

What do you think of when you read the word cling? It's more than just holding something. I think it's holding something fiercely that supports you that you just don't want to let go of for fear of falling. As a person with a history of bad knees and lack of stability, I am always searching for support, sometimes without even knowing it. When I walk, I constantly scan the floor for wet spots or ice so that I can think proactively and quickly locate the nearest support. Most often, it's my husband's arm that instinctively goes up so I can hold on and navigate my way without harm. It's such an automatic response for me to seek support, as automatic as breathing. Is it that way in my spiritual life as well?

In my first fifty years, I had a number of losses that, like falls, could have and should have knocked me to my knees. At first, I had to think about whom I was going to cling to for emotional support during those times. Oftentimes it was a family member or friend, but they didn't always know or understand the depth of my grief. My people were not omniscient and without knowing the whole story, they didn't always have the right words to keep me from falling down a dark hole. Over time, I have learned to cling to the Lord. I know there are sure to be rough patches ahead in this next stage of life, but just like breathing, I want to cling to the Lord as an automatic response. And although the path I am walking will never be easy, I can be assured that He will never let me fall.

Dear Lord, We often cling to You and Your word in times of stress, but please help us to maintain that fierce hold on You during periods in our life when we are relatively stress free. We climb these mountains to pursue You. And even when we aren't actively seeking You, we know You cling to us—we are Yours. We are so thankful for that bond. In Jesus' Name, Amen

Date of Hike:

Climbing Party:

Notes:

WILSON PEAK

"I'm alive!" That was all our climbing partner wanted to hear. He and a friend were attempting to summit Wilson Peak, one of their first 14er efforts. When the Class 2 hike turned into Class 3 climbing, they made the decision to return to their camp at Silver Pick Basin. They could see the tents down in the valley. Rather than return by back-tracking on the trail that they just ascended, they decided it would be faster to go down on a 1,000 foot snowfield. With no ice axes (they readily admit they were inexperienced and "stupid"), they picked up a couple of dagger-shaped rocks to help them slow their speed as they glissaded. Glissade is defined as to slide down a snow-covered slope without the aid of skis. Our friend made the sledding run and stopped with no problem before the slope turned from snow to rock. His climbing partner was not as controlled or lucky. He slid down the slope and attempted to stop his acceleration by digging his feet into the snow. But with so much momentum, he flipped over, head first, and crashed into the rocks. He immediately stood up and declared, "I'm alive!" Amazingly, he had no broken bones. He just needed some stitches in his fingers and elbow. It was a good lesson—it's imperative to practice glissade self-arrests and to always know how the chute ends.

Let the mountains bring peace to the people,
And the hills, in righteousness.
Psalm 72:3

This summer, my heart has been racing and not in a good way. I am in a season of life where I thought I would be slowing down. Instead, about three years ago, I ventured into several projects that seemed to be going nowhere, but have all ramped up in intensity this summer. Projects that on the onset had little hope of ever coming to fruition are suddenly bearing fruit—all at the same time. These are good things, but even the best of things can cause stress. As they are all screaming for my attention simultaneously, I am losing focus and am struggling to take these projects across the finish line.

And then she texted...a friend proposed a trip to the mountains. And my soul sighed because I know the mountains are the one place I can get some rest. Cell service becomes spotty, taking away distractions, and the mountains quickly remind me of the smallness of my projects and worries in comparison to the grandeur of my God. With that perspective comes a peace—a peace in knowing that He is God and I am not—and all is right in my world.

Dear Lord, please help us to keep our eyes on You. When the rest of the world tries to invade our lives with demands, pressures, and expectations, let us be still enough to hear Your voice. We know there will be steep slopes filled with rocky distractions trying to divert us. We long to know where You want us to place our spiritual gifts and energies. Guide us as we strive to live each day in a way that most glorifies You. Gently nudge us to the path You have set for us. In Jesus' Name, Amen.

Date of Hike:

Climbing Party:

Notes:

WINDOM PEAK

• •

Besides safety, there is very little that can make my husband turn around when he climbs a 14er. He is equally as dedicated to his training hikes. With that said, as we were preparing for a hike up Windom Peak, there was one workout we abandoned because of a very unusual problem. The trail was completely covered with cobwebs, wet and sticky in the morning dew. Having never encountered this extreme, we kept pushing on in the early light. But it didn't get better. It was the strangest, most eerie phenomenon. We switched places so I could lead, but this did not help, as I'm nearly a foot shorter than he is. His facial hair caught every strand until he couldn't take it anymore. As he flailed about, the dance moves he showcased were nothing short of impressive. We abandoned our dawn hike in the woods and waited until later in the day when the "cobknockers" had cleared the trail. We learned whoever is first to wake up and start hiking usually ends up clearing the trail of spider webs for everyone else. The combination of sticky webs and the uncertainty of what might be entangled in them made for a very unpleasant hike.

Therefore, since we have so great a cloud
of witnesses surrounding us,
let us also lay aside every encumbrance and
the sin which so easily entangles us,
and let us run with endurance the race that is set before us.
Hebrews 12:1

When reading this scripture, I have always pictured myself near the finish line in the marathon of life. I can hear spirit voices of all of those who have passed on before me cheering me on towards completion. Somehow, the entanglement of sin was less obvious to me, which is so reminiscent of the cobwebs on a mountain. We often don't see the sin or situations that we find ourselves tangled up in until it is too late. We find ourselves in a sticky mess that gets us off our path and often causes us to stumble. Like the cobwebs, sin can be nearly invisible to the naked eye. We think we are walking on the path of righteousness until *"gotcha!"*—we find ourselves in a mess. Maybe if I listened intently to what the great cloud of witnesses was saying, I would hear, "Don't go that way...don't step there." Perhaps they would be speaking from experience, trying to knock the cobwebs out of my way so I wouldn't stumble through the same webs that they had found themselves in. I am grateful for the "cobknockers" in my life and hope I listen more carefully to the wisdom they want to share.

Father, this should be simple, but it's not. Don't let me get entangled in my own sin. Search my heart. Convict me of the sins I might not even see. Give me eyes to see and ears to heed the warnings. Help me not get snagged in a web of deceit—even if it's a web I have created myself. In Jesus' Name, Amen.

Date of Hike:

Climbing Party:

Notes:

Date of Hike:

Climbing Party:

Notes: